# *FROM PAIN TO PASSION*

## *THE JOURNEY OF SELF-HEALING*

Lauren Van Kas

www.trafford.com

North America & international
toll-free: 1 888 232 4444 (USA & Canada)
phone: 250 383 6864 ♦ fax: 812 355 4082

# *Introduction*

Thank you for purchasing this book. For whatever reason, you were drawn, attracted or intrigued by it and I am grateful. I believe that almost everyone in the world wants to experience a greater sense of peace and ease in their lives as well as desiring greater positive passion.

Since the age of fourteen I have been writing; first songs and poems, then on to journaling, business briefs, reports, procedure manuals and now my first instructional book that encompasses my own personal journey. I trust that I have written enough about my life in these pages to illustrate and demonstrate how you have the ability to create your own healing.

This book had a journalistic quality to it while I was writing it for I was and still am on my own personal journey of self-healing. Just because I wrote this book, does not mean I now have all the answers and am completely healed. I still feel my emotional wounds at the most unexpected times and am stunned at their power and intensity. What has changed most significantly for me since the year 2000 is that now I am able to identify quickly when a wound has been touched and how to regain my emotional balance more quickly. I am also experiencing more joy, happiness and passion now, than I ever have in my conscious past! True joy and passion are most often experienced at the time we are born up to about the age of one or two. After that we begin to be programmed by our external environment. I have literally spent about 40 years living unconsciously with this programming and not knowing why I was so unhappy and not getting the results I said I wanted.

It is very important for me to state this book is not about blame; blaming others or myself. I totally love and accept all the people in my life for who they are. I'm very clear that my parents did the absolute best they could with the knowledge they had at the time they raised their children. It is my most heartfelt intention that people will release their pain and move to healing through the exercises listed. I wrote the following with the intention of assisting others by telling them my story and what worked for me through all the years I've spent reading, studying and learning.

At age 38 I finally began to live my life on purpose. I am now clearer about who I am, what I'm doing and how I might change my thoughts, feelings, words and actions so that I will realign myself with my Highest Purpose for being on the planet quickly and effectively. These shifts have an immediate and direct outcome on my results. I trust that this book will assist you also in this regard, however, please know that at the conclusion of this book, the journey of healing continues.

## _Acknowledgements_

The support, encouragement, mentorship and inspiration of several people have assisted me in writing this book. From my most essential self, I feel extreme gratitude and love for the following people.

Gerrard is at the top of my list; my friend, companion, best friend, and husband. He is known more affectionately as Gerry, Ger and Ger-Bear. Gerry has lived with me for the past 28 years. Not unlike other couples living together, we have experienced the entire rainbow of emotions with each other. We've gained tremendous amounts of information and knowledge by being in each other's lives.

What first drew me to Gerry was his amazing gift of speech and conversation. Able to speak intelligently on a wide range of subjects, I became intrigued by him and wanted to know more and more. So rare had it been for me at the age of 19 to meet a man who was willing to engage in conversation before any other kind of activity!

Our friendship began, developed and flourished. We share our entire lives, thoughts, feelings and many activities with each other. No one else knows me so intimately. All my assorted and sordid secrets from the past have bubbled to the surface next to his nurturing presence. This man has stood in the face of all my storms, (which have been many) and barely flinched or blinked an eye. A few times he's had to leave the room or the house for a short time, but he always came back.

Gerry, you are my rock. I doubt very much that I could have come so far in such a short time without you being so inextricably a part of my life. Thank you for being with me, my love, my soul-mate.

There is another very special man in my life. Christopher is my very wise and gentle 19-year old son. This young man burst into my life with a warrior like cry that stunned me with its bass sound during my drug-induced stupor in the delivery room! I was so surprised to hear that I had a son, as I somehow felt sure I was going to have a girl. I've never for a moment regretted that he was a boy and in fact am really grateful, as his energy in the male form is such a good match for me. I had wanted my own child since I was ten years old. At 28 years of age I was finally holding my very own bundle of love and I honestly could not get enough of him. I spent the first four and a half years with him, day in and day out, barely allowing anyone else to care for him. As the years have passed, I've watched my dear son change and grow into an amazing young man who is strong and capable in the world, yet tender and loving with animals and young children. Christopher is wise beyond his years and has actually been coaching and mentoring me since he was about 10 years old. I'm amazed and so grateful to have such a loving son. Thank you, Chris.

Next, I thank Arlene Rannelli, my first teacher in self development. Arlene is an amazing woman. While short in physical stature (well at least compared to my height of 5'10"), she is a giant in insight, compassion, love and encouragement. She has led thousands of people through the Context Series of courses and now has developed and delivers her own course, "Mastering Your Essential Energy".

Check out the website: www.masteringyouressentialenergy.com. Arlene has a presence that immediately compels people to listen to her. She is commanding, powerful, thoughtful, intelligent and respectful of other people; respectful in such a meaningful and loving way, that I model myself after her. Thank you, Arlene, for your perfect blend of encouragement, curiosity, solid steadfastness and unwavering belief that I am capable of creating my own magic.

Nadia Wnuk, my teacher, mentor, friend and soul sister. We shared so deeply with each other in such a short space of time. I'm still amazed today at how quickly I trusted you. Nadia, you have the ineffable quality of leading with conviction, strength, purpose, generosity and love in such a way that people are drawn to you like a magnet. Every time I see you, I'm content just to be in your company, especially when you have a goal. I love to watch you in action. I feel so inspired in your presence. Thank you for your trust and love.

My dear sister, Henriette has always stood by me. When the going got tough I knew I could always phone her and receive positive encouraging support. The process of reviewing this book with my family was very challenging as we do not view life in the same way. Henriette was also kind enough to offer her services as editor, reviewer, and advisor after I received the third proof and found more errors. It's been a long haul to get this book complete and out to the public and I thank her for being there for me. You are such a sweet angel of a sister.

I also have a huge group of friends that have loved me, put up with me, listened to all my dramas over the years, and I feel such huge gratitude to each and every one of you. You all know who you are, so please know how much I love each of you. Other dear friends that I thank are Sandra Higgins, Jessica North-O'Connell, Laura Bentley, Barb Singer, Anne Sands, and Robyn Unwin. I could write paragraphs of your names, so if you don't see it here, please realize I do honour and respect you. Thank you all very much for your support and love over the years.

T. Harv Eker. Without you, I would not have written this specific book. On February 13th, 2003 I attended your "Train The Trainer 2" course with Peak Potentials in Vancouver, BC. Through one of your exercises I was able to come up with my nine chapter headings, and 45 sub-headings, 5 per chapter. From there I was able to springboard right into writing. Harv, I also thank you for having the courage to do and be what you are. Your courses are absolutely amazing! Another mini-commercial, check out www.peakpotentials.com and sign up for the Millionaire Mind immediately. The first time I saw Harv was at The Millionaire Mind and I loved him! He spoke what I thought and felt and I laughed out loud so hard. It was like, "Yeah, baby! Right on! Tell it like it is!" Harv is a tremendously gifted speaker and facilitator. Combining humour, logic, intelligence, research and insight, Harv was able to come up with a series of courses that leave people wanting more and more. Thank you Harv, for the gift that you are to the world!

# CONTENTS

# Chapter 1    DISCOVER YOUR WOUNDS

## Review Your Life

Many of us are clear that we have experienced wounds in our life. We feel pain as we relate to each other. What is often not clear is where the pain originated. What caused it? When did it start? This is why it is so important to review our lives. Not just from a mental point of view, but rather writing out the major pieces or events that we recall and also going back as far in time as we remember.

Some people choose to review their lives from the present backwards - year by year or decade by decade. Others find it easier to start from their earliest memory and move forward. Still others prefer to start with the most vivid memories and then move around from there. The method is not necessarily the most important thing. But do begin and write them down. If possible, beside each memory write the year or approximate age you were at the time of the event.

I would strongly suggest you do this now, before reading any further in this book. The pencil icon below is repeated throughout this book and it always follows a direct suggestion to do a writing exercise. I have written the book intentionally with exercises so that you will experience the full benefits of bringing forth the knowledge you already have stored in your subconscious.

Now that you have written out your memories, let's talk about patterns. The most obvious place to look for patterns is in our relationships. Do you see any patterns or similarities in the events that you have written down? If not, what is the nature of the events? Are they the most exciting moments that you recall? The most dramatic? The most emotional? What is the specific nature of their significance

Write out your answers to these questions now.

At this point you will have written out either the patterns or the common themes that occurred during your most vivid memories. Let's discuss emotions, since that it the crux of what this book is about. The word emotion evolved from the Latin word "motus", meaning "movement or motion". When we experience emotion, we feel energy moving through our bodies and minds. The nature of the energy usually relates back to one of our earliest experiences.

For example, let's talk about shame. I recall moments of shame when the kids I went to school with made fun of my dad. My dad's back was humped quite severely from an early age. He suffered scoliosis of the spine and had very poor nutrition during the war. As an adult his back was very malformed. Kids described my dad as "the Hunchback of Notre Dame", and other negative terms. I felt embarrassed. I remember how my face turned very red and hot. I wanted to crawl under a rock. This was one of my earliest memories of shame. I began to resist how my father was and wanted him to be different so that kids wouldn't make fun of him, and I would feel more accepted by others.

Several things were occurring during this experience. I felt the emotion, experienced physical discomfort and made some mental associations with the whole experience.

Another example I recall is when my dad bought a small tape recorder and each of the three oldest girls in our family were encouraged to individually sing into the tape recorder. When it was my turn, I sang a verse from the Christmas carol, "Away in a Manger". When I finished my older sisters laughed at me and made critical comments about the way I sang. Inside I felt myself shrink. I was mortified, embarrassed, humiliated and knew from that point forward that it was not a good idea for me to sing out loud by myself. I so wanted to be accepted by my older sisters. They were my role models and I wanted to be like them.

As I review more of my life memories, I see several patterns emerge. One pattern related to my belief that I wasn't good enough the way I was. I didn't fit in. I was an "outcast" – "different", "weird". In "Maslow's Hierarchy of Needs", the Social Need described as the sense of belonging is critical in all situations whether it's our family, school, church, work, sports or academic teams - anywhere where a group of people come together.

Another pattern emerged through my happiest moments. The pattern had to do with self-expression - the arts, leadership, being on stage performing. I know now how essential it was for me to get the attention, recognition and acknowledgement for what I was doing and what I had achieved. Another one of Maslow's Hierarchy of Needs, is the Esteem Need. The most important piece that was holding me back from full creative self-expression was my self-limiting belief that I was not good enough, that I would not be accepted or valued. Do you see how these two patterns I uncovered fit together? I was looking outside of myself to my social situation for my esteem.

Let's go back to your list of patterns and themes. Don't try and determine whether or not, your pattern or themes fit into Maslow's Hierarchy of Needs. Simply write a few paragraphs about the themes and patterns you uncover and how they have influenced your life. It would be most helpful for you to consider the uncomfortable times in your life, when looking for patterns or themes as this will go a long way towards moving from pain to passion to peace. In fact, if you have not done so already, I suggest you make two lists of patterns. One list would describe the happier more joyful circumstances in your life and the other list would be those situations and circumstances when you were sad, uncomfortable or depressed.

Now that you have written out your most vibrant memories, the theme or pattern that flowed through these memories and the influences they have had in your life, did you experience some insights or epiphanies that give you greater clarity into who you are now?

It is possible that you may have suppressed some seriously sad, painful or unpleasant memories as too difficult to deal with, let alone write about. In which case, this book may not be your best avenue for moving forward. For others, you may want to do this book at the same time as working with a counselor, coach or other advisor. If you feel certain that what you have written thus far is a strong representation of you and what your life has been about thus far, congratulations! I encourage you to continue.

I would like to reassure you that writing to yourself is one of the safest ways to explore who you are, how you came to be the way you are and what, if anything you want to do from this point forward. If you are feeling very uncomfortable about writing the most intense times of your life, consider whether speaking with a professional counselor, therapist, psychologist or psychiatrist is a more appropriate avenue for you to explore yourself.

We are now going to begin the next section, which may be like visiting an old friend, but seeing them in a new light. For other people this section will be new and somewhat uncomfortable. If you proceed with the belief that at the end of this book, you will feel lighter, happier and more confident, it will be easier to keep moving forward. Remind yourself of this as you feel tempted to put the book aside or convince yourself that this is really not what you want to be doing right now. This is your critical self trying to prevent you from changing. You would not have attracted this book into your life if it was not the best thing for you at this particular moment.

Most important be gentle with yourself. It is very hard to move forward in life when our own inner critic is using up all the "air-time" so to speak and never gives any other part of us an opportunity to speak.

Directly from the mouth of T. Harv Eker, one of my teachers, I would suggest that when this critic speaks, you say, "Thanks for sharing", and continue on.

### Trauma

It is very possible that at this point you may have already written about one or more traumas that occurred in your life or that you may uncover them as you proceed through this book. Traumas are an important cornerstone of how we have built our lives to this point, so I am now going to spend some time looking at it.

The dictionary definition of trauma is: "Morbid condition of body produced by a wound or external violence; emotional shock".

Trauma shows up in a variety of ways. The simplest one to see is in our physical bodies, based on a physical wound. A car accident for example may leave us without limbs, fully functioning body parts or scars. The origin of emotional, mental and spiritual trauma is much more difficult to trace. The results of these traumas may also manifest in many different manners. I have seen the result of emotional abuse show up in someone who is extremely shy and unable to speak up in groups. I have also seen it show up in people who stutter. Sometimes the manifestations are of a physical nature and sometimes they are not.

The most valuable principle to understand here is that it is essential that you become aware of what your traumas were. I trust that you were led to this book because of wounds that you want to heal, which means at some point you experienced either a trauma or several traumas. The awareness that you gain about yourself is critical to moving through pain.

Take some time now to write out a list of what the traumas were that you have experienced in your life to this point. After you have composed the list, go through them one by one and write out as much as you remember of what you were experiencing "EMOTIONALLY" during the trauma and after the trauma. Please do not write out a history from a thinking point of view, e.g. "I thought he should have known better. He should not have been drinking, etc., etc." This will not serve you at all. It is essential that you talk about your emotional state only. For example you might write, "I felt (use a "feeling word") such as sad, scared, depressed, worried, lonely, etc. beside each of your traumas that you experienced. Begin now.

You may have written out several pages at this point or even just a few paragraphs. What we are striving for is that you begin to access the emotional reactions you were experiencing at the time of your trauma. You should now have a black and white version of what this looks like. Some people find it easier to draw, sketch, doodle, paint or sculpt their emotions. For our purposes, I believe this book will serve you the best if you first write about your emotions. The other expressions of emotions are equally valid, but I recommend they be done separately from this book.

Now that you have a list of your emotions, it is time to move into the next topic.

### When Do I Feel Pain?

I would like you to consider the word pain in both its physical definition and emotional definition. Take some time to think about instances that occur in your day-to-day life when you experience the sensation of pain.

For reference purposes, the dictionary definition of pain is "Suffering, distress, of body or mind."

Many of us feel pain listening to others describe their life story, or watching a sad movie, seeing the commercials for World Vision, or reading a book. The list is long and varied. Please write your own list and be as detailed and vivid as possible, so that you will see a very clear picture of when it is that you experience pain. Begin now.

Now look for some similar themes or patterns. If you are able to see some, write out what the patterns are. Take time to acknowledge that these are very important to you and that you have stored this information in your subconscious for a real and valuable purpose. It may be that you have learned it is necessary to protect yourself against possible future pain, so your emotional antenna responds to a certain kind of stimuli. Appreciate and thank yourself for doing this.

## *When Did the Pain Start?*

This next section may be a little more difficult for some. I want you to trace back the origin of your pain. This may require a bit of thoughtful contemplation or meditation. Read the following over and then try it.

Put on some very quiet and peaceful music. Lie down on your back without any of your limbs crossed and close your eyes. Or sit in a chair, again without crossing any limbs and close your eyes. Take several very deep breaths, feeling your stomach expand as you breathe in and then slowly breathe out until there is no air left in your lungs. As you are breathing, tell each part of your body to relax as you breathe out. Begin with your feet, then slowly move up your body and include each section. For example, feet, shins and calves, knees, thighs, buttocks and genitals, belly and lower back, waist, chest and upper back, shoulders, upper arms, lower arms, hands, neck, head, and face. When you have gone through your whole body, continue to breathe slow, even breaths. Say to yourself, "I am safe and secure. I will protect myself. I will look after my own well-being. I am safe." Continue breathing in a slow and even manner. If you feel yourself tense up somewhere in your body, take your attention to that place, and tell it to relax. When you are calm and relaxed you are ready to proceed.

Ask yourself the question, "When did my pain start?" Do not try to think up the answers, or stress yourself in any way. Simply allow the information to come up, acknowledge it by saying, "Thank you". Then continue to ask, "When did my pain start?"

Continue breathing. It is very normal for people to experience tears, sobbing and shaking. For some this is the first time they have given themselves permission to look at where the pain has started. When you feel you have accessed all the possible places in time that the pain started, open your eyes and write down as much as you recall of the information your subconscious provided you with during this exercise.

When you have completed all your writing, you may wish to consider taking a break. You have done some amazing work up to this point. Congratulate yourself. Do something you enjoy. A bath, a hot fudge sundae, a walk - whatever it is you like to do that you consider a treat. When you return we will begin the last section of this chapter.

### *How Does Pain Affect Me?*

This section is very valuable because you are going to learn how the pain you have experienced up to this point in your life has affected you on various levels. It is most likely that if your pain was of a physical nature, it affected your mobility or physical ability on some level. If your pain was more of an emotional, spiritual or mental nature, you are going to uncover not only its physical effects, but possibly how the experience of pain has conditioned you to set up some limitations in your life.

For the purposes of this book we are going to focus on the pain that was an emotional, spiritual or mental experience. During our first encounter with emotional or mental pain, we often feel a sense of shock - "this isn't happening", or "what's going on?" We feel frightened, threatened. We may even believe our lives are in peril. After the trauma has passed and we begin to recover, our body goes through a series of reactions. First, as I've already described, we experience shock, then often disbelief, followed by hurt, anger and resentment. We then begin the process of scarring, those thick layers of hardened skin that indicate where a wound once existed. This is the physical manifestation of scarring. Mental or emotional scarring has layers of defensiveness that are hard to penetrate. Scarring has often been mistakenly referred to as "healing". Healing will only occur when there is forgiveness. We will discuss this in further chapters. Right now, we are going to continue with the reactions of shock, disbelief, hurt, anger, resentment and scarring.

During the anger and resentment stages, we begin to list the warning signs of how the pain occurred. Often this is followed by self-recrimination. Such as, "I've should've seen that coming" or "Why didn't I run away or fight back". The lists of self-criticisms might be very long. In essence, these criticisms are also useless. Self-criticism is another form of finding fault with self, when in fact you are not to blame, but are rather responsible only for your reactions. The fact of the matter is, the trauma did occur, we did experience it and now we are left with how we will react to it.

The most common reaction is to develop a form of scarring that includes layers of aloofness, shyness, lack of self-confidence, bullying and other forms of anti-social behavior. This is how we learn to keep people away from us and in turn avoid any future pain. However, this kind of behavior also prevents us from experiencing friendship, love and intimacy with other people.
This kind of living leads to feelings of isolation, loneliness and depression. Ask yourself the following questions and write down the answers.

1. Do I have deep, rich and fulfilling experiences with other people in my life?
2. Are my relationships with other people of a short-term basis (less than 1 year) or a long-term basis (more than 1 year)?
3. Do I consider the people in my life to be acquaintances or friends?
4. Is there someone in my life I call when I feel lonely, afraid or nervous?
5. When something good happens in my life do I celebrate with others or by myself?
6. How do I spend my birthday, statutory holidays and vacations?
7. How do I feel when people praise me? Do I thank them or try to diminish their compliment somehow?
8. How do I feel and act when people give me attention, especially in group situations?

Now that you have written down the answers to these questions, consider whether you have allowed the experience of pain to dictate how you interact with other people in your life. This would include people in your family, neighbourhood, school and work environment. If you have more to write on this subject, do it now.

## Chapter 2    *UNLOCK THE PAIN*

### *Creating Safety*

At this stage of the book you may be thinking, "Wow! I've done a lot of work. I think I'm good now." Yes, you definitely have done a lot of work, and please continue. We have just begun, literally. What you do from this point forward may dictate the level of success you begin to experience in all facets of your life. Do you want to improve your relationships, your success at school and/or work, your success with money? If you answered "yes", to any of these questions, it is important that you continue reading the rest of this book and doing all of the exercises.

Before most of us try something new, we want to know that we will be safe, both physically and emotionally. The feeling of safety allows us to experiment, to push ourselves a little harder then we normally would.

How do we create this safety? Choose a physical environment that is safe. This includes a secure home base. Choose to be around people whom you think nurture you. You will want a place where you will not be interrupted by loud noises. Turn off your phones, find a quiet room, open or close the window coverings – whatever creates a greater sense of calm and safety for yourself. Perhaps you would like just a little light, like that of candles or small lamps.

Each person's "safe environment" is as unique as the individual. Experiment with different types of settings to see what is most comfortable and comforting to you.

### *Choosing Your Support*

When all of this is secure and you honestly believe you are in a place that is stable and safe, you will be in a better position to proceed to creating emotional, mental and spiritual safety. Ensure that you are surrounded by people who love, honour and support you. These cannot be people who criticize or demoralize you. Choose people in your environment who support your decisions to improve your life. The most supportive people are those who are willing to risk upsetting you by telling you when they think you are trying to coast, or not live up to what you said you wanted to do and are willing to demonstrate 'tough love'.

Some of us, and I definitely include myself, are masters at convincing others that we are working hard, taking risks and living courageously. The truth of the matter is we may be fooling everyone and ourselves, and worst of all, we are ripping ourselves off by not living up to our fullest potential.

It is imperative that the people you want close to you love you enough to give you really honest feedback. These people will be very clear with you about what you want and what kind of support you require, based on what you ask for. Support comes in many different forms. It could be a weekly phone call, a lunch, a visit - the form is not the important piece. What really matters is what works best for you and then *ASKING FOR IT!* Make sure you are very clear, direct and specific in your directions. Pick people you know who do what they say they will do. Do not pick a procrastinator or someone who is part of a "mutual back-sliding party" where you all sit around consoling yourselves and each other by saying "It's alright. We're busy. We'll do it next time. You deserve a break. Etc. etc." This is not the kind of support I'm talking about.

It's challenging enough to break out of a pattern, without surrounding yourselves with people who want you to stay the way you are; people who are insecure, who do not want you to change. If you change, they may start looking at themselves and for many people change of any sort is extremely uncomfortable.

### Staying Connected

The reason I have written about support in the above paragraphs is to emphasize the importance of staying connected with other people during your life; especially during difficult transition periods. It would be easier to return to the way we have been doing life in the past; easier not to look at the pain, re-experience the feelings, relive the memories.

But you would also stay stuck! If you want to feel the deep, burning passion of being alive and what it is to be overjoyed at being on this planet, stay connected with people.

If you are of a shy and retiring nature, this might be the most challenging piece; however, it is essential. I'm not saying that you have to throw parties and become the next socialite. But you do need to leave your house. Go to the library, coffee shop, bookstore, church, synagogue, temple, computer store, grocery store - wherever you will have an opportunity to see others and talk to people. If you have friends that you think would provide the kind of support described above, call them. Even if they are people you have not talked to in a long time; send them a letter or email. You'd be surprised how thrilled people are to hear from friends out of the past!

Maintaining relationships and friendships takes effort. Don't expect others to do the work. If you want the relationship, you need to put in the time and energy to make it happen. If the other person is not interested in maintaining a friendship, you will know that soon enough as they won't return calls or initiate any kind of getting together. In that instance, let the person go and focus on others.

Think about what your interests are, and then find organizations, clubs or places where groups of similar minded people congregate. None of us live all alone on an island. We are all together on this planet for a reason. Take advantage of the gifts other people are willing to share with you. I truly believe every person is here for a purpose, has gifts to share and is an expert is some capacity.

Take a few minutes right now and write down your interests and where you could meet like-minded people. If you have friends you have not contacted in some time, but would like to reconnect with, write down their names. For those of you who already have people in your life who will support you in the method I described above, write down their names.

## Allow the Process

During the reading of this book and most often while you are doing the exercises, you may experience a wide range of emotions. Please don't censor yourself. Everything you are feeling is real and valid. Give yourself permission to feel, think and be whatever comes up for you. Have compassion for yourself. For many the depth of emotion that rises to the surface is difficult to comprehend. Allow it to be. Don't immediately begin to analyze and criticize yourself. When you are able to do so, write about your thoughts and feelings. There will always be time later to analyze what it is and how it came to be, etc.

Other people in your life may have some preconceived notions of how you should behave, speak, think and feel. This is especially true of family members. Remember that they are speaking from their own minds experiences and what may be true for them is not necessarily true for you. Your family likely wants only the best for you; thank them for their opinions and then do what is best for you. I am absolutely certain that you have all the answers for what you want inside you. You need only to ask, and then have confidence to believe in your answers. Who is in a better position to know what is best for you than you? No one else has walked in your shoes, thought your thoughts, or felt your feelings. Trust yourself. Believe in yourself. All manner of good things will follow from there.

## Give Yourself Permission

At a very early age, we learn to contain ourselves - to reframe how we are being into something more palatable and acceptable (and we are told "better") than how we truly are. This is generally a crock of horse dung! We were born pure, innocent, and beautiful. Our behavior is learned. We absorb all kinds of information from our early environment and use this information as our blueprint for living.

Later in life we discover that everything we learned is not necessarily working out for us. We may feel unfulfilled, sad, lonely, desperate and afraid. We are not living 'on-purpose' and with passion. I will talk more about this in later chapters. For now, I want you to write down on a blank piece of paper and in large handwriting.

## "I GIVE MYSELF PERMISSION TO THINK, FEEL, SAY AND ACT WHAT IS TRUE IN MY HEART. I BELIEVE I AM A DIVINE SPARK, PURE AND INNOCENT AND AM HERE FOR A REASON!"

This does not mean you are giving yourself permission to hurt others or take advantage of people. This permission is in relation to how you more fully participate and express your ultimate potential. It's important to stop cutting yourself off from fully embracing yourself and life, if you have been doing so to any degree. This is why it's so crucial that you create safety for yourself. Life is your stage and you get to set the content, write the story, pick the cast, paint the props, direct the show and be the star.

There are a few more pieces to learn before this will happen. Otherwise, I would have finished the book here!

## Chapter 3     *FORGIVE THE PAST*

### *Whose Approval Do You Want?*

This may sound like an odd question. Generally, we would say "No one! I am my own boss." Take a moment to think back in time and really consider this question. Who do you recall that you wanted to be pleased with your efforts? Whose attention did you want? Whose love did you bask in when they were happy? Can you think of times that you felt a glow of pride for an achievement that was acknowledged by someone? Who was that someone?

Most of us will be able to uncover one person, if not a series of names. Write these names down now.

Consider why you wanted or perhaps still want their approval. Write down any answers you come up with.

Review your answers with this thought in mind, "Is it possible to give these feelings, thoughts, ideas and opinions to myself?"

If yes, how would you do it? It is important that you put strategies in place to give yourself the acknowledgement you want and need, because without strategies, you will do yourself a disservice by reverting back to looking to others to give you what you want and need. Contemplate the idea that other people's opinions don't matter. Each person lives inside their own head and creates their life from their own dreams, hopes and wishes. Since we are all so unique, how is it possible that one person's opinion be worth more to us than our own? It is inexplicable when we really, deeply think about it. I am really the best person to measure myself. I know when I am working hard, being honest with myself and others, keeping my word and living life to the fullest. Yes, acknowledgment, recognition and attention do feel good to some of us when we receive it. However, when we determine that our own happiness is dependent on outside circumstances and people, we may be setting ourselves up to be the victims of circumstance, another person's good or bad mood, rather than being in charge of our own lives. How much more beneficial and rewarding it is to be in the driver's seat and give ourselves acknowledgment and approval when we really deserve it.

Self-approval is not bragging or going out and buying ourselves all kinds of trophies and rewards for the things we do in life. Physical items may be a reminder to us to feel good about ourselves, but they cannot provide the feelings on their own. That comes from within us. It is quite often a deep, fulfilling inner experience. I'm sure you would agree that life is sometimes a bit of a merry-go-round. We go around and around, without stopping to get off and celebrate what we have achieved. For some, the ride of life itself is a challenge. Many of us have extremely busy lives and within this busy-ness we create our own obstacles to climb or go around. Let's not forget to say, "Good job!" when we do surmount the obstacles and barriers. Especially when it's something we feel resentful about doing, such as when I have set a goal for myself and then discover it's harder than I thought, or I'm not in the mood, or whatever. And I do it anyways! That's an important moment to say, "Well done! I'm not a quitter. I have accomplished something I wanted and I'm proud of myself for doing it."

Perhaps you are thinking, "Well, that just sounds silly. I'm not going to start talking to myself. I don't need that kind of self propping-up." If you are thinking thoughts like this, I challenge you to try it out first. Then decide whether you need, want or desire to approve of yourself. For some people this will be the first opportunity they have ever had to really experience the value of self-love. Trust me, it is very worthwhile. Until I started to do this for myself, I never truly experienced the depth of self-love I have today. In fact, I usually felt inferior to others; never quite measuring up to what I perceived was their expectations of me.

This started with my parents and teachers and continued through my working life. The moment I began turning inward for approval rather than outward to others, I saw myself in a new way. I began to have compassion for myself which also manifested as more compassion for others. I began to trust my instincts and intuition and discovered I was pretty terrific! I stopped believing the messages I received early in my life of "not being good enough", and

16

reprogrammed my mind to say that I was good enough, in fact, most of the time I was doing very well.

To get to the point where other peoples' opinions don't matter, don't affect you and are just background noise, is a very freeing, self-honouring moment. I'm not saying I'm completely unaffected by others. At times I do consider what they say to see if it has any merit or relevance to my situation. More often than not, I discover that I'm usually in the best position to determine my value, my contribution and my substance as a human being. Other people are coming from inside their own minds and quite often what they think has nothing to do with me, and everything to do with them. Really, unless I ask for another's opinion or thoughts, what they think is none of my business.

### When Trust is Lost

Just thinking about the word "trust" conjures up all kinds of thoughts. The Concise Oxford Dictionary dedicates almost half a page to the definitions of trust. The words that come readily to mind for me are faith, belief, reliance and responsibility. I knew from an early age that I did not trust easily. Hidden behind a façade of friendliness and openness, I reserved judgment about people until I had time to assess whether the person was worthy of my trust. I had a series of unconscious tests that I put them through and they either measured up or fell short. More often than not they fell short, as my standards were extremely high. More importantly, since I was doing this unconsciously, people had no way of knowing what my standards were. I never verbalized them. My thoughts were, "Somehow they must know!" I don't know what I was thinking… that perhaps they should be psychic? Who knows?

Between two and four years of age I had a life experience that practically destroyed my ability to trust. The incident involved a very close relative who I had put complete trust and faith in. Since the incident happened at such an early age, I didn't have a memory of it but was told about it when I was about 18 or 19 years old by an older sibling. At the time of hearing the story, I was dubious it had occurred, but since my sister is 6 years older and had such a clear memory of it, I began to believe her. In 2000 I was doing a workshop and saw the pattern that emerged from that event.

In the early sixties, my Dad worked a lot. They had four children at the time, with a fifth on the way and my Dad quite often worked two jobs. Usually he came home tired, ate a meal, rested a bit and then went back out and worked some more. One day I was sitting on my father's lap playing and talking with him. We were joking around and having a good time when suddenly my mother commented that my father spent far too much time with me. Something else about how he was spoiling me and it wasn't healthy. My sister didn't recall the exact words my Mom said only that she was very annoyed with my Dad. After Mom had finished her tirade against my father, he picked me up bodily and flung me across the kitchen where I hit the wall and sank crying to the floor. He then said to my mother, "There, is that better?!?!? Are you happy now?!?!"

Even as I write this now, I'm crying as I think of that tiny little girl so happy one moment with her daddy - loving him and him loving her and then suddenly being thrown away like a used dish rag. "What had I done to create this rage? How could he turn from me so quickly? Stop loving me so suddenly. Did he now hate me? Why did he hurt me?" Oh, how sad and lonely I must have felt; confused, frightened and so totally alone.

I know there were other instances of my parents punishing us with various implements, but this event was a turning point. Please bear in mind, that today I harbour absolutely no resentment against either of my parents. I may not agree with their form of punishment, but at the time they were doing what they thought was the best thing to raise us properly.

When I was 38 years old and began my own personal journey of healing, I recalled the telling of this incident and I had an epiphany. I realized this incident actually occurred and that a pattern began that day. For approximately 40 years I had been living unconsciously without trust. I never totally believed people, especially anything they told me. It was, "yeah right, that's what you say, but what are you going to do? Show me, don't tell me."

So how did I move forward from this place, you may be thinking? Well, it's an excellent question and the true cornerstone of my own ongoing healing began at that moment. The crux of what I learned was about self-trust.

The little girl who had been cast from the lap of love, took this message into herself. "I am unlovable. I am not worthy. I have no value. People will always reject me. Why even try?" I went from a very outgoing, happy-go-lucky child to a placid, quiet, reserved person with brief moments of spontaneous emotion that I quickly shut down if it was met by disapproval. This became my mold for how I lived my life from that point forward.

The lesson that I learned on that day, long ago was to be very careful of how I expressed myself; always adjusting to fit in, to be liked, to be met with approval. I began to deny my very essence. Of course this created a lot of nervous tension and fear inside of me. I never believed I could really get along in this world. I would always have to be cautious and careful. My most base understanding was that no matter what I did, even if I did meet with another person's approval, I couldn't really believe them for sooner or later they would discover my flaw of being unlovable and reject me. What do you think the chances were of completely loving another or being loved for an extended period of time? Well, if you said not very good, you're right.

I dated frequently and with many different boys and young men. Flitting from one to the next, I was full of reasons and excuses why they were never good enough. But the truth was I didn't trust myself and projected that onto them, so that in my conscious mind I was saying they could not be trusted, they were only after one thing, didn't really love me for who I was, etc. etc. On and on it went.

Even when I was married at 24 years old, I held on to this belief system. I spent many years of my marriage holding back from fully loving my husband and myself. I always made sure I kept something in reserve, just in case. I made sure I was always on the offensive in terms of love and warfare. What I mean by that is I always had my arguments and reasons lined up in case I ever decided to leave the relationship. In fact, leaving the relationship was a thought I often had

19

during any type of conflict. Anything my husband did that was not totally accepting of me just proved that I was right about people always rejecting me, even if they said they loved me. After being married for fourteen years, I realized it was time to start loving myself, believing in myself and most importantly begin trusting myself.

When I did this, I began to risk. I tried new things. Things that I always wanted to do. My life stopped being about what others would think, whether they would approve, find me acceptable, or want to spend time with me - in essence, whether they would love me. I see now what a truly losing proposition it is to live my life trying to please others. I will never be able to please everyone. It was important that I start the journey of healing with myself. When I'm living in harmony with what I truly want, I exude a happiness and confidence that is attractive and draws people to me.

### Reawaken the Present

When I use the words "reawaken the present" what I'm talking about is waking up in the present. It is so easy to spend most of our time thinking about the past and the future. I know I catch myself constantly using the past as an excuse for why I'm thinking and behaving in the manner that I am now. It goes back to trust. If I'm really trusting myself, which includes honour and respect and listening to the soft quiet voice inside of me, I will always be behaving in a manner that is in integrity with my essence.

All any of us really have is right NOW - this moment, this instant. Nothing else exists. The past is a memory and memories have been known to change based on input provided by others. The past is not fail-safe. The only thing I might do about the past is change my mind about how I view it now. I might use the past as a way of learning - learning what worked for me, what doesn't work for me. The future is totally unknown. It's a dream that I create from my imagination. The future beckons like a warm, gentle beacon promising all my heart's desires. I'm not sure if this is true for you, but for me the future is where I'm constantly drawn to living. It's the place where everything is better. I have more money, less debt, more freedom, happiness, opportunities, etc. The real drawback about living in the future, though, is that I'm not there now nor am I here, living my life in the present. I'm not loving where and who I am right now, in THIS INSTANT! Do you see what a trap it is?

When I'm totally engaged with my present moment, my soul sings. I feel the food I had for breakfast stowed away comfortably in my tummy. The food is becoming fuel as I write this word and I now have the energy I require to sit here with focus and write. I am experiencing gratitude. I'm feeling rightness in my world. I'm thrilled that I have good health, the money to purchase food and shelter. I have real love in my life, a loving and forgiving husband who adores me, a beautiful, healthy, clever and talented son who chose me to experience his life with.

I see that what I'm doing right in this instant is what I have been dreaming about for years. Sure, not all the details are exactly as my imagination would have it, but like an artist, I fill in the details as I go along. I've always wanted to write in my own home, working on a book that is important to me and one that I trust will have value for others, such as you.

I would like you to stop reading now and write down all the different things and people that you are grateful for right now in this moment.

### The Beauty of You

I fully realize that this will be a very sensitive subject for many and it doesn't matter whether you are male, female, young, middle-aged or older. Everyone I have met has their own personal and subjective opinion about what beauty is. For some it is what they see, for others it is more of an internal experience - something they feel.

For this exercise, I want to focus on you. My purpose is not to convince you of what I think. I only want to share my experiences with you in the hope that you will have an opportunity to see how what I write might fit you. All I suggest is that you consider what you read, try it on and see how it fits your life. I believe that every person is beautiful. Sometimes I don't see their beauty right away, but I've

21

found (and I *absolutely swear this is true!*) that by believing in their beauty, it shows itself. Sometimes the beauty shows in a smile, a touch, something I see on their person initially, but usually, what is more true is that I get to see the beauty of the person in their behavior.

I believe we are all connected to each other. The threads are invisible, but in my mind's eye the threads are silver and shimmer. While they stretch like elastic bands, they cannot be broken - ever. I also strongly believe the Great Divine resides within everything and everyone, and yes, this includes plants, animals, rocks, etc. Some people refer to the Great Divine as God, Allah, Jesus, Buddha, Source Energy, Great Spirit, etc. It is not the name that we give this force, but the essence of the Divine that is of an all-encompassing importance. As each person is born, the Divine shows itself and everyone is attracted to the person, as if by an unseen magnetic force.

I fully comprehend that life's early experiences, environments and situations colour people and affect who they become as adults. However, we are all born equal in that we choose to believe whatever we want. It is the belief system that forms us into who we are at this moment. It is my privilege in this lifetime to see people as a beautiful gift to the world.

As Marianne Williamson wrote, "... as I give myself permission to shine, so do I give others that permission to shine also." The light that shines from inside of us is the Divine, our life-force that keeps us connected to each other and this planet.

When you too believe in your inner beauty, that you are here for a reason, that you are an incredibly amazing and beautiful being, you will be able to accomplish ALL YOUR HEART'S DESIRES!! It is the strength of our convictions and our beliefs that get us through anything and everything. It is not the amount of money we have, our talents, friend or families. They're important but not everything. The most important piece is YOU and how *you view yourself.* I cannot emphasize this enough. You are the source and everything in your life begins with you; your thought processes, your beliefs and opinions *CREATE THE LIFE YOU HAVE NOW!!*

Many other authors have written on this subject and to some degree, many people already know this. When you truly understand it and take this concept into your soul, you will soon see that you have incredible power and control over your own destiny.

The next writing exercise is to write down all the things you want to do and experience that you have not yet done. This will be a list that you might refer to over and over again over the years. Title it your "Wishes to Manifest Into Reality" list. Begin writing your list now.

My wish is that through this book and through synchronizing with other people of like mind, that eventually everyone will believe the concept that you create exactly what you want in your life. It begins and ends with you. Once we stop blaming others, our parents, our spouses and partners, our jobs and the world at large for what we don't like in our lives, we may choose to think about what we do want and really begin to make changes. By focusing on ourselves and accepting our beauty, we are much more willing to see the beauty in others.

### *Accepting Others*

I realize this is a huge challenge, however by starting with loving, embracing and accepting myself, accepting others is easer. By embracing (not necessarily physically!) and accepting others I find my life runs easier and smoother. By fully loving and embracing yourself and believing in the beauty that is you, you will discover an amazing result. Suddenly you will have much more patience and tolerance for others.

One important piece of information that I learned from my friend, Arlene Rannelli, is this - each person in the world is behaving in a way that they believe is truly "lovable". The way they are behaving is the way they were taught by another, usually a parent or authority figure. Or they may have picked up the behaviour somewhere along their life's journey. We are the sum of our experiences, plus much, much more. I do believe in reincarnation and I believe we are all the sum of all of our lives' experiences. This belief system explains so much to me. It also assists me in accepting others.

Here is another gem that I learned from other writers and facilitators. "How someone else is, has nothing to do with me". Sounds simple, doesn't it? But say it over and over to yourself. "How someone else is, has nothing to do with me. How someone else is, has nothing to do with me. How someone else is, has nothing to do me." I've discovered that this type of thinking allows me to have more tolerance for other people's behaviors. When I am not taking other's people's words and behaviors personally I am much more accepting of how and who they are.

I like to believe that I have the power to influence other people's thoughts or belief systems however it is each individual's choice to make the final decision as to what they ultimately think, believe and do. Each of us is in charge of ourselves. As soon as I grasped this, I was able to be happier in my life. The concept of believing that "I decide my own behavior, thoughts and beliefs" is extremely revolutionary and controversial to many people. You are probably thinking, "Yeah, well how is this true with kids? Doesn't what I say or do have an impact on how they behave?"

I find this topic extremely interesting and initially I want to say yes, as a parent, what I say or do to my child does have an impact on his behavior. One thing to remember though, is that children are extremely adept at managing their behavior and other forms of communication to be in alignment with what they want. If a child wants love and acceptance, they will adjust themselves to get that, no matter what form it comes in. This is true of abuse and other negative forms of attention that they somehow construe as a form of love. However, that is a whole other topic that I will discuss in Chapter 8. Suffice it to say that at this point in the book, I want to emphasize that other people "CHOOSE" their behavior, thoughts, feelings and actions. Not always from a conscious point of view, but they do choose. Very young children operate from what I believe to be a very primal place. It is a place the brain identifies as survival. Even a baby learns from birth what crying will get them. This is an emotional place for me. So I know I need to write about it.

As a child I often heard my parents say that parents should not immediately respond to a crying baby and often if you let them cry long enough they will stop. When I heard that everything inside of me wanted to shout, "No! That's so wrong! A crying baby is using its only form of communication to convey something to the parent."

As a child, I did not know how to articulate to my parents those opinions without it becoming a power struggle. From the time I was a baby I learned not to cry if I needed something. Tears were looked down on, derided, chastised and criticized. I found other means of communicating. But picture it for a moment - A new baby, freshly born from a womb where all of her needs were looked after, suddenly needs something and makes a noise to attract attention. It might not be a physical need the baby wants, sometimes they are lonely or afraid. That noise comes in the form of a cry. The cry gets no attention, so it becomes louder and louder. Still no attention is forthcoming. Now the baby is crying in total earnest, her little face all red and squished up. Water is running freely from her eyes and nose and she's probably soiled herself from the intense physical exertion of crying. Still there is no one coming to care for her. Eventually due to sheer exhaustion the baby stops crying. What has she learned?

I learned as a baby that I was alone. I was in physical discomfort, pain, afraid, lonely and there was no help forthcoming. I had only myself to rely on for what I needed. To look at this from a positive perspective, I would say I learned independence early. From a negative perspective, I could say I learned I could not rely on others. Either way the experience formed me. It also gave me the opportunity to accept or reject my parent's opinions and behaviors. Intrinsically I knew my parents did not have the answers I needed. As a child, teenager and young adult I rejected most of what my parents thought, as it didn't gel with what I thought or believed to be true. I was labeled "difficult" and "rebellious". Even though I was reacting unconsciously, I knew I was the best source for my answers. This reasoning process relates back to the baby I was and the programming I received when looking externally for help and answers.

As the person I am today I am much better at accepting my parents. I understand they are the people they are based on how they were raised, the environment they grew up, the religious convictions they chose to adopt and many other criteria too numerous to list. They did the best they could with what they knew. By having accepted them as different people than I am, I am free to love them and accept them as they are. Even more importantly, I am no longer looking for their approval and love for me. It is no longer a part of my survival. It is wonderful to experience their love, but not absolutely necessary for me to be. This is so freeing. When I pull this attitude into all my relationships, I feel better about myself. I still live within the confines of my culture and have respect for others and their way of being, but I don't constantly find it necessary to adjust my behaviour in the way I did as a baby and a child.

## Chapter 4    RECOGNIZING YOUR PERFECTNESS

### Connection to the Divine

Like everything else I have written, I don't ask that you believe me, I only suggest you consider these ideas, try them on, wear them for a while and see how they fit. They may not fit you at all, in which case you won't keep the ideas. However, it may surprise you that what initially did not seem right to you, may change and become something else within the confines of your own life's experience.

Now is the time to write down your concept of the Divine. This would be the essence of what you consider to be your source of life. Also write down where and how you came to feel and think this way. If you don't have any religious or spiritual inclinations, simply write the word Divine and then as your writing exercise, write all the words you associate with the word Divine.

Now that you have completed this exercise, your mind is probably in a place of considering "Why am I here? What is my purpose or mission? Why is the world here?" These questions will probably lead you to other books and sources of learning and I suggest you be open and curious to see what kind of experiences you will attract to yourself. Be open to any form of teaching or teacher, as they come in many different guises - young, old, male, female, different races and religions. We are all teachers and students to others.

The purpose of this book is not to provide you with the answers to all your questions. I only have my own answers, just as you have all the answers to your own questions. Sometimes other people, books or teachers simply remind us of that which we already know but have forgotten.

This exercise may have awakened in you the concept that you are a part of a whole, a sum total that is greater than you on your own. The universe is vast and great and, while we are these tiny beings that are a part of it, so are we a universe unto ourselves. Each person is in a constant state of recreating themselves, and so impacts others and their environment, whether subtly or dramatically. None of us are invisible or without impact on others and in turn on the world at large. I say this because I believe that by impacting one other person, the ripple effect is started and continues in an ever-expanding outward wave.

## The Perfect Universe

My purpose in writing this book relates to peace - peace within myself, yourself and peace in the world. I'm trusting in my mission statement, "I create peace in the world by teaching people how to heal themselves so that they live in their highest power and join the force for peace." My book provides exercises and tools for you to utilize in your own journey of healing, which I truly believe will assist in creating world peace. As individuals begin self-healing, their awareness about themselves, others and the universe around them increases which helps to heal the world. I know we have this power of healing when we are in touch with the Divine that is inherent in each of us. The beauty, the Spark of God, Mother Nature, Mohamed, the Goddess, Buddha, Krishna - the name doesn't matter - only the acknowledgement and awareness that we are each of us, so much more than what we see in the mirror - our own mirror and the mirror that others provide when they reflect us back to ourselves.

When you look at a flower, a tree, a blade of grass, a sunset, a mountain range, a desert at sunrise or sunset, animals and all other forms of nature - do you see flaws or do you see perfection? I see the perfection. Would it not stand to reason that we, as complete natural beings are also perfect? Even with our self-perceived flaws, wounds, scars, and mini-imperfections, does it make us any less whole? Why do we perceive these things as if they were imperfections?

Life's circumstances are just that; circumstances. The situations that we attract to ourselves are just learning experiences. Why is it so necessary to make them black and white, or even more importantly, right or wrong? This kind of thinking has not aided us in our development or evolution! If anything, this kind of thinking has kept us where we are! Why do we feel so compelled to apologize, to excuse our behavior and for some, even our existence? Are we any less than the trees, the stars, or the animals? I think not.

Honestly, all of creation is equal, complementary and intertwined. As I gaze upon the faces of people walking by me, I see them as my sisters, brothers, parents - in essence a part of me. I am not a scientist. There are others more adept than I at explaining how the molecules and atoms of the world are connected and interdependent on each other.

I once heard the expression that the taking of a life was like killing a universe. This struck me at such a core level. I understand it to be true and one step beyond. Killing something is like killing myself. The killing of a bug is like killing the tiny, vulnerable part of me that is simply seeking existence. Who am I to end that life? What right do I have? I'm sure I could find all kinds of reasons, excuses and justifiers for killing a creature that could bite me or harm me in some way. How much more difficult would it be to find a way to coexist? This seems to be such a challenge. I know there is a way. Perhaps I will have the opportunity to learn about it and write future books.

The part of the world that people will inexorably argue is not perfect is mankind's obsession with war. This is such a huge subject; one I do not feel I might even begin to encompass in a few paragraphs. I'm sure that many of you will agree that all of us are composed of light and dark, good and evil, right and wrong, kindness and harshness, generosity and greed. The list could go on and on, but I think you see my point. No matter what opposites I describe though, it's really about balance and choices. Would you agree that at any given point we are at choice, at choice about our reactions, our thoughts, and our feelings? If you do believe you are at choice, does it not follow that you are also at choice about how you want to be in this world?

Other people are always giving me the opportunity to choose how I want to react in a given situation. Let's take driving for example, since so many of us do it. When someone cuts me off without signaling and to such an extreme that I must brake or I would risk slamming into them, I am at choice about how I want to react or behave. On a good day, I generally just brake and don't give it a second thought. On another kind of good day, I consciously think to myself, "It's okay, Lauren. You don't know what's going on with that person. They may just have received news that they have cancer or someone they love has died. Let it go. It's not worth obsessing over."

If I'm in a negative mind frame on the other hand, I would probably honk my horn, and yell something. I'm not proud of the fact that I lose my cool from time to time. But given that my mission statement relates to contributing to peace in the world, which reaction would you say would be closer to doing that? Not a tough guess, is it?

I used this example to demonstrate how even in a minor regular everyday moment, all of us are at choice about which side of us we want to express. Many people would find it a bit difficult to swallow that their thoughts, words and reactions have an impact on the world around them. Yet, this is exactly what I am purporting to say.

Right now is the time to write about your universe. Describe the world around you, your own personal environment, city, home, work or school life, your friends, family, and economic situation as you see it.

Now that you have completed the writing exercise, take a look at the adjectives you have used to describe your universe and ask yourself if they are the words that accurately describe how you would want others to describe you. If not, consider what you would want to be different and write about that. Additionally, write out in positive statements exactly how you would like your personal universe to be. By positive statements, I mean only use affirmative statements such as "The house is..., the garden is..., my street is..., my health is..., etc. etc." Do not use any language that contains negatives, such as "I don't want" or "I hate..." etc. etc. In fact, any time you think of a negative statement, turn it around into a positive or affirmative statement and write that instead. For example, I might think "I don't like front yards without sidewalks and grassy boulevards separating them from the road." From that I would write, "I like front yards with sidewalks and grassy boulevards that lead to the road." Notice how I eliminated the negative words and replaced them with positive statements. Please begin writing about your own ideal personal universe now.

# Mirror Reflections

The universe is continuously mirroring back to us what we put out, including our thoughts and feelings. I wish I had the ability to explain it in scientific terms, but then again, if that is what you wish to know, I'm sure you will find other sources for this explanation. I have seen how this reflection works. For example, just recently I was thinking to myself, "I would really like an opportunity to do some more facilitating. I want some experience to put on my resume that will assist me in attracting more facilitation experience." I didn't say anything out loud; I just thought these thoughts quietly. Two or three weeks later I received a phone call from the president of a company that I had done volunteer work for over the past three and a half years. She told me she had a proposal for me. Would I be willing to do some "paid", and I stress "PAID" facilitation work over the next couple of months. It was exactly what I had been thinking about. Of course I said yes!

Saying 'yes' to what I asked for is an important part of the reflection/manifestation/creation process which I will talk about later in more detail. For now, I want to emphasize the idea of how our thoughts create our reality and the importance of acting on what the universe provides to us when we ask for it. This is part of the belief system that "I am my word". Whatever I put out to the world, in thoughts, feelings, words and actions, comes back to me. The universe will also notice if I ask for something and then turn it down when it shows up. This is telling the universe that I wasn't serious or I didn't mean it when I asked for whatever I asked for. The universe will then stop providing me with what I want. Sending out double messages, one positive and one negative, is confusing and the universe will not supply anything as the two thoughts also cancel each other out.

The reflection process also works in relationships. When I choose to believe that a certain kind of relationship is difficult, I will receive all kinds of evidence to support me in this. As an exercise, write down some of the names of people you find difficult to be around. Include the reasons why this is so.

Now that you have your list, review it and make note of any patterns or similarities.

Next, write up a list of people who are easy, pleasant and enjoyable to be around. Beside their names write down the qualities of what it is you like about them or the relationship you have with them.

Look at this list to determine if there are any similarities and if so, make note of them. Look at both lists and honestly assess whether the qualities or traits are qualities or traits that you possess. Be honest. If you see some qualities in people from both sides, that you know you yourself possess, write those down now.

The purpose of these exercises, as you may have guessed, was to see how the people we attract into our life mirror ourselves.

My thoughts and beliefs, which are again entirely mine, about this concept are this. I believe we attract certain people into our lives to mirror and reflect us so that we might choose to grow and evolve as human beings. This is entirely about being aware and conscious. If I am choosing to be unaware, I might just explain away these unpleasant people in other philosophical terms. However, then I risk missing the opportunity of learning not only about myself, but also risk not learning more about others and the world at large. I enjoy and am always in a state of learning about how we interact and why we do the things we do. This is an absolutely fascinating chance to see the really BIG PICTURE in life. I catch glimpses of the magic and the mystery, the poetry and perfection and the mystical dance of which we are all a part.

### Recognizing the Perfectness of Others

The beauty of this kind of thinking is that I am now free to see how beautiful and perfect other people are. I'm not talking about the kind of perfection that stems from doing everything "right". That is perfectionism, from which I am still recovering! It's an ongoing process, this recovery business! Striving for excellence is so much more rewarding and easier than striving for perfection as a form of "rightness".

When I talk about how perfect others are, I mean it in the sense that we are all born beautiful and perfect, beautiful, a spark of the Divine. Just like the birds, flowers, trees, ocean, blades of grass, forests and sky. Are they not exquisitely crafted and a wonder to behold? We too are a part of this magical place called earth and are just as perfect as they. If you hold the following thought in your mind and speak it aloud (and I invite you to repeat it as often as you want), you will soon notice the change in your perception of the world and all of the people in it.

# "I am a perfect Divine Spark. I was created perfect and my mind and body, soul and spirit, are perfect exactly the way they are now!"

I think it is critical that you really emphasize the "NOW" part as many of us, including myself think we need to be different. Different hair colour, eyes, nose, teeth, breasts, penis, less weight – whatever. The minute and I mean the absolute moment, that we get how beautiful and perfect we are now, the sooner we will feel happier, more at peace and joyful with each breath we take. It matters not whether we look, act, or think like the people we put on pedestals – it is who we are at our essence. The more I am accepting and loving of myself at my core, the more I see myself as beautiful and perfect on the outside. Others may judge that I am overweight, have less than perfect teeth, or whatever, but I experience a greater sense of peace and happiness than I have ever felt before. This began as I learned to accept myself as I am, now.

When I was a very young child, the kids at school teased me relentlessly for years – calling me all kinds of nicknames, such as "Bucky", "Beaver", "Bugs", "Buck-Toothed Beaver". I felt shunned, out of place, a complete misfit. My parents couldn't afford braces and I thought they were the ugliest teeth in the world. Yet it didn't stop me from dating or making friends. The people who got to know me, saw past all the things I thought were flawed or "imperfect" about me. Now I realize how I became very self-limiting based not only on what I thought were my physical flaws, but also my inner flaws. And here is where we get to some really interesting ideas.

To begin with, let's do another exercise and this is important so please follow these instructions carefully.

Take out a blank sheet of paper or turn to one in your notebook. On the left-hand side of the page write the title "Physical Flaws" and underline it. Then below that title, write in a column, one below the other, all of the physical flaws you think you have and number them. So, mine looks like this:

<u>Physical Flaws</u>

1. 20 pounds overweight
2. Buck teeth
3. One eyebrow higher than the other
4. One eye smaller than the other
5. Poor posture
6. Feet too big
7. Thighs too heavy
8. Etc.

Write down as many as you think of. When you have completed your list, you will be ready to read the next set of instructions.

Now on the right hand side of the page I want you to write the words "Results of Belief Systems" and underline it. Take a look at the list on your left and look at the first item on your list. Think about what prices you have paid for this belief about yourself. What are your results from holding that belief system about yourself? Write a number "1." underneath the words "Results of Belief Systems" and start writing down all the thoughts you are having about your first item. Do this for each of the items on the left hand side of your page. As you are doing this exercise – it will look something like this.

| Physical Flaws | Results of Belief Systems |
|---|---|
| 1. 20 pounds overweight | Didn't want to dress or undress in front of my husband. Lowered my desire for sex. Stopped wearing my favorite clothes. Stopped feeling good about myself. |
| 2. Buck teeth | Withdrew from large groups of people. Thought of myself as less than others. Became defensive, withdrawn and hurt. |

Continue through with all the items you have listed.

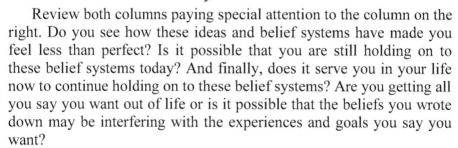

Review both columns paying special attention to the column on the right. Do you see how these ideas and belief systems have made you feel less than perfect? Is it possible that you are still holding on to these belief systems today? And finally, does it serve you in your life now to continue holding on to these belief systems? Are you getting all you say you want out of life or is it possible that the beliefs you wrote down may be interfering with the experiences and goals you say you want?

If any of this rings a bell with you, it is important to decide what you want to do about it.

Take some time to journal about your thoughts.

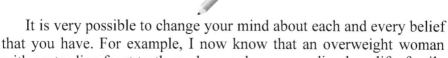

It is very possible to change your mind about each and every belief that you have. For example, I now know that an overweight woman with protruding front teeth can have a deep, rewarding love life, family life and a rich and satisfying career. What I've just recently started thinking is that it is also possible for me to have a public life; a career of performing music and facilitating and keynote speaking. I don't need to look like a model or actress to live out all my passions. These were preconceived notions that had no base in reality.

### *We Are All Created Equal*

Yes, I'm sure that many of you have heard this phrase before, used in all kinds of different scenarios, such as church, school, new-age disciplines. What does it really mean and what impact do those words have on me, if any? This is the question that may be uppermost on your mind. I know that it certainly was for me. I could find all kinds of proof that knocked this concept. For example, how could a baby born to extreme affluence be equal to a baby born in a third world country suffering poverty, drought and famine? Obviously, one would have much more of an opportunity to succeed, let alone live.

What is of importance at this stage is not the economical or environmental circumstances into which a person is born, but what exactly they are born with. What does each person have inside of them, and I don't mean physically. I am thinking more about character, personality, thoughts, wishes, beliefs, dreams, and ideologies. It wouldn't be difficult to argue that all of these items are actually formed as a baby grows. They pick up their ideas and beliefs from their parents, environment, school, church, friends, etc. Personality and character is a whole other subject that I may explore in another book. Suffice it to say that at this point, I'm quite convinced that our personality and character are pretty much what we're born with. It's all the other influences that we allow to form and change us along the course of life.

When I use the phrase, "we are all created equal", what I am saying is that all of us are born fresh and new. All of us are children of God, Nature, the Universe, the Great Spirit, the Divine. Children of God are Divine Sparks. I honestly believe that all babies are angels here to remind us to feel hope, joy, peace and love. As they look at us with their trusting eyes we see only acceptance. Their eyes and their trust were once our eyes and our trust in the universe we were born into. In this way, we are all the same.

We all have the same right to live, breathe, eat, dance, sing, work, and play. Finding our voice in this is sometimes a little more difficult. But it is definitely our Divine right to have, be and do all that we want that is not harmful to ourselves or others. Don't ever believe anyone who tries to tell you different. It just ain't so! And what is most critical of all is that if you believe you have the Divine Right, it will become manifest and truth for you in your life.

# CHAPTER 5    TURNING PAIN INTO PASSION

## What is Emotion?

I have heard emotion described as "energy in motion". While that sounds great, what does it really mean? Energy I understand to be a force, whether physical, mental or emotional, the force is quite often palpable to us as humans. The "in motion" gives me the sense that not only is the energy not still, but that it is *continuously* in movement. The Latin root word to emotion is "emote", meaning to give expression to. Putting these thoughts together means the movement of energy through expression, whether through art, music, verbally or even in actions.

Another definition is the idea of emotion being an "agitated mind, feeling, or excited mental state". This is very clear to me because I know that for me, emotion follows thought. Usually some kind of data or information comes into my mind and I filter it through my view of the world. When the data meets up with all my preconceptions, that is when my thoughts are either of acceptance or resistance, the resistance usually results in some kind of emotional reaction. This is when the "energy in motion" concept kicks in.

One of my strongest reactions occurs when I perceive something to be unjust. It might be the words or actions of another. Somehow, somewhere I feel wronged, betrayed, misunderstood and before I know it, I am in a full-blown emotional state. This is where a situation might become dicey. At this time, when the emotion is running high, the brain is shouting "Fight or Flight." It is difficult to remain rational, yet we must find a method or process whereby we remove ourselves, physically and or mentally from whatever the situation is and take some time out.

Quite often I find it most beneficial to talk with friends and family. They are not close to the situation so are more objective. I pour out whatever is going on for me and get some feedback. This also gives me a chance to calm down in a safe environment, gather my thoughts and strategize about what I want to do next. Is there an action to take and if so, do I want to take that action? I believe it is critical not to take any action while in a highly emotional state, as I have observed that I never get the results I wanted. However, after taking the time to calm down, look at the situation from as many angles as possible, and talking to others, I am then usually better prepared to see where I want to go from there.

I really want you to get that I believe in the power of emotions. Anger quite often is the face of hurt. Hurt hides behind anger, because anger is stronger and more powerful. Our western society does not honour the emotion of "hurt". Many of us recall experiences of feeling "hurt", yet few people if any were given tools on how to express feeling hurt in a non-threatening or non-judgmental environment. Expressing hurt was often derided as being weak. The expression of anger on the other hand, quite often gets us results even if it is not always the exact results we want. Expressing anger feels more empowering than expressing hurt.

When I feel extremely angry about something, it means something needs to change. And I don't always mean that it is something outside of me. It may be me that needs to change. My attitude or belief system could be getting in the way of my fully comprehending a situation and how it actually affects me directly. I may be acting out a past behaviour pattern, not consciously recognizing the state I'm going into as a pattern.

The power of emotion helps us to change. Change is an inevitable force of nature, a universal law. Just look at the seasons! Nature reminds us of what we are. To be still, unchanging is to be dead, stagnant and rotting. We're either growing or dying. The choice is up to us.

I so believe in the power of emotion to be used for a productive means to an end  When strong emotion comes up for you, rather than labeling it as something bad, look at it as passion – a powerful ability to express. This is the secret of turning Pain into Passion. All of the answers to our questions are inside of us. Through quiet introspection or meditation we will hear the answers to all our questions.

## Uncovering the Depth of Emotion

Just writing this heading I feel a deep sense of anxiety building in me, as I imagine it may do for some of you too. The word "uncovering" suggests that I am about to reveal something that has been covered or hidden to this point. It is so amazingly synchronistic that I just completed a weekend doing exactly this. The course was entitled "Mastery" and it was all about self-expression. I discussed my fear of financial destitution and poverty. The facilitator then instructed me to spend the rest of the weekend as a "street-person" or "bag-lady". I was further instructed to be dirty, not to change my clothes, wash or brush my teeth. I had to act crazy and beg for money. At first I felt resistance and then I decided to get into character. The second day I was challenged to be "desperate" instead of crazy and to stop asking for money. This is when I felt myself turn inward. My desperation up to that point had always been silent – locked away in a tight, small space inside of me. Now I was looking at it, feeling it, living it. It was an emotion that I had up until then, kept "covered".

I felt the anxiety, the fear slipping out from my well-covered depths and moving through me layer by layer. The challenge given to me by the facilitator was to assist me in getting more real and more in touch with my emotions around poverty. It worked. I was very miserable. I didn't express my usual joy and passion for living. I felt sad, lonely, alienated – not a part of the group. I recalled many instances in the past when I had experienced similar feelings. It didn't feel good, but by then I was so immersed in my "muck" that I couldn't pull myself back. At the time of writing this section, it has now been three days since I returned and I still feel my emotional self stuck in the mire of desperation.

What is most amazing is how that desperation switched to anger. The anger was directed at myself, my parents and my spouse. I couldn't believe that I was 41 years old, didn't own my own home and was $54,000.00 in debt. How did this happen? I am now at a place of turning that around and changing my direction.

You now have an idea of how I uncovered an emotion that was necessary for me to look at to change my life direction, It's begin to address how this would look for you. First of all answer this next question. Don't read ahead until you have an answer to the question and write it down. The question is, "What do you want out of your life?"

Think about this next question seriously and deeply consider your answer before writing it down. It may actually become a list and it is very important that you not stop writing until you have the entire list completed. The question is "What has stopped you?" or more accurately "What have you allowed to stop you from getting what you say you want?"

Do not read ahead until you get the answer or answers to this question all written down.

You should now have an answer of what you say you want out of life and a list of what you have allowed to prevent you from getting it. This is a comparison of values. Up to this point you see that you value your list or reasons of "why not" more than you value what you say you want. Be honest with yourself. Do you really want what you have written down or did you just write something so that you could say you did the exercise? This is not a game. This is your life. Be serious. Be thoughtful. Consider what moves you at a very deep level and what you feel will make you say at the end of your life, "It was all worth it. I got to live everything I said I wanted. I thought it, felt it and was it. Yeah me"!

Do you want to change your answer at this point? If so, redo both questions and when you are finished, we will move on.

Most likely you have experienced a myriad of emotions during these exercises. That is good! It may not have felt good at the time. But this is what we're aiming for – uncovering emotions. I'm sure you think about things and the reasons why you do them. The most valuable reason for uncovering emotions is to be conscious of them. If we are not conscious, our unconscious thoughts rule our actions which affect the results we get in our life. Being conscious takes effort and work. I'm not saying that I'm conscious at every given moment, but I am a work in progress. I also believe this is true of all of us. We are all works of art in progress, just as we are all Divine sparks of God. And yes, I do believe we were created whole and perfect. It is only in our judgments and the judgments of others, that we start believing we are imperfect and need fixing. Never forget that judging says more about the person judging than the person being judged.

Another reason or purpose of why it's so important to uncover buried emotions is that once we are conscious of our emotions we may choose to look at them and decide if we want to keep using that emotion in an unconscious way.

When I did my work at "Mastery" I brought up the emotion of anger. A deep, dark, and desperate face of anger that I disliked and did my best at keeping tucked away. I still have difficulty using the power and passion of anger in a constructive way. Since my first memories and thoughts, I have seen the negative affects of anger and how it has been used to destroy. I'm afraid of my rage – it seems so immense and unmanageable. Somehow, when I'm in anger I feel like it has all the control and takes over. When I'm in a rage, I see only red and my own righteousness; all else fades to the edges of my consciousness. My fear is that my anger might destroy all the good that I have built in my life. However, and this is a big HOWEVER, I am now so conscious of my anger that when I feel it building inside of me, I am more at choice about whether I want to give that anger the freedom of expression or whether I want to re-channel that anger into something else. The most valuable lesson I've learned is that I do not have to be at "the effect" of my anger. It doesn't have to rule me, or blindside me, or take center stage. Instead I have the choice to state coherently to another when I am angry and move forward from that position.

This position feels much more powerful as I have my conscious awareness and control. This is true of any emotion. It could be grief, despair, loneliness, emotional pain, sadness, fear, loathing, and frustration. It matters not what the emotion is, only that we gain clarity of it and bring it up from our depths to look at and see what role it is playing in our life. How does it show itself? What prompts it into action? Where did it start? Is it useful in my everyday life or is there an opportunity for me to express my emotion in a time and place that will be most beneficial to me? You are in the best position to answer these questions for yourself.

## *Pain and Passion Distinguished*

Here are two words that often are found traveling hand-in-hand. They are frequently used interchangeably, but actually mean very distinct and different things. First, let's look at some dictionary definitions for them and then we'll do some exercises and have some more discussion. Well, I'll actually be doing the discussion, unless you chose to talk to your computer screen or page!

**Pain**: punishment, penalty; suffering or distress of body or mind; also: a basic bodily sensation marked by discomfort (as in throbbing or aching); great care.

**Passion**: strong feeling; also: the emotions as distinguished from region: RAGE, ANGER; LOVE; also: an object of affection or enthusiasm; sexual desire.

Under the definition of pain, we have distress of the mind. Under the definition of passion, we have the definition of RAGE, ANGER and love; all emotions that affect us on a deep level and all emotions that are often associated with distress of the mind. Now you see how easily these two words, "pain" and "passion" become linked.

Somewhere along the evolutionary path, humans have attributed the passion we experience to have an emotional context; a framework, foundation or container for holding our emotions. The intensity of passion when experienced negatively, is usually turned inwards against ourselves, and becomes a source of emotional pain.

Are we able to experience passion without pain? I think it is possible. Once again though, it requires us to be conscious. It is so easy for me to turn my passion against myself when I am not getting what I want, because what I want is dependent on others. This simply sets me up for falling into a "victim pattern."

Many other writers and researchers have done huge amounts of

43

work around the victim/master philosophy. Essentially though, any time I feel at the mercy of the world, situations or other people, I place myself in a victim situation. The moment I put myself at the beginning of a typical "victim" statement, I then become the master of my own destiny and this all ties in with the pain/passion subject.

Bear with me as I make this transition. So, a typical "victim statement" might be something like, "He makes me so angry when he doesn't follow through with his promises." Change this into a master statement by simply changing and adding a few words such as, "I feel so angry when he doesn't follow through with his promises." I am now the master because I am at choice about whether I want to feel this way or not. Yes, I may initially react with anger, but then with consciousness, I get to choose whether I want to continue feeling this way. This is where the passion/pain dilemma comes in. When I operate from the victim mentality I am inevitably going to experience the emotion of pain because I've chosen to allow others to be in charge. I've allowed other people's behavior to dictate how I'm going to feel. This takes me out of the driver's seat or master position and puts me into a passive/bystander/victim role.

Passion, as you will recall, states that I have a strong feeling. At the precise moment I have that feeling, I GET TO DECIDE, (as in Master Position) whether I want to suffer or be in distress. Even more importantly I get to decide whether I am going to be at the mercy of my emotion. When I am conscious I choose to get at the source of my emotion and change its direction into something more positive, more constructive. Generally I choose action over staying paralyzed by my emotion. I get out of the passive mode and decide rationally, "What do I want?" "How do I achieve what I say I want?" This all comes from a place of knowing I cannot change others, but am always at choice about changing what I'm doing, thinking and feeling. This is such a powerful place.

Let's do an exercise to put these concepts into a more tangible form.

Think back to a time where you experienced intense "negative" emotions that ended with a result you did not like. Write out this experience in as much detail as possible. Include the setting of where the incident occurred, write out the dialogue and write out what was happening inside your mind, any physical reactions you may have experienced and what feelings you were having. Be as honest as possible. This writing is not for anyone's benefit but yours. Trust me, I know all about not being completely honest. I'm practiced at holding back myself and it has taken great discipline to not hold back; getting past the fear of being judged helps. No one will judge you. Should you choose to share this writing with someone and they do judge you, remember their judgments say more about them than you, right? Now begin writing out your incident.

At this point you should have written out your experience. Perhaps to some degree you relived it. Writing is extremely cathartic and beneficial on many levels. Allow yourself this opportunity to heal as this book is all about your personal "Journey to Healing".

Now let's look at what you've written. Look for any phrases that are accusatory to others in nature. Sentences such as, "He/She made me....", or "he/she did this to me...", or any other kind of statement that suggests someone else other than you, had the power to influence your feelings, thoughts or actions.

After you reread these statements (the ones that are blaming others), write them down the left-hand side of the page in a column. When this is complete, go through each statement one by one and identify the feeling you have as you experienced it, either back then during the time of the incident or now as you read it. Write down these feelings on the right hand side of the page next to each relevant statement. When you are complete, look at all the comments on the left-hand side of the page. Begin writing now.

This next exercise is going to take some concerted effort and imagination, but I know you're up for the task. You've come this far, so keep going. What I want you to do is change each statement so that you are the responsible one. For example, my first statement would read.

"He makes me so angry when he doesn't keep his promises."

Anger/Frustration - The emotion I'm feeling now as I read this statement.

The new sentence reads, "I feel so angry when he doesn't keep his promises." Do you see how the responsibility of the emotion moves to me?

Please write out all of the new statements for your old statements.

Now that you have completed this exercise, do you see how the point of focus is away from blaming the other person and you get to take control of the situation by seeing that you get to choose how to control yourself? The situation is just that, a situation. Everything is neutral until we give it meaning.

Using my example once again, the situation is that he didn't keep his promise. End of story. But this is where "my story" begins. I've been raised, programmed and conditioned to believe that people should do what they say and what they promise. People who don't do what they say they're going to do are bad people. They're not dependable or reliable. I can't rely on them. I can't trust them.

Now here's the big question. Why do I feel "angry"? Well, this "he" is a person in my life that I've chosen to be with and he is not behaving in a way that fits in with my programming, so he must be at fault, because my programming somehow became about me being "right". I mean, what kind of person am I if I have faulty programming? Well, that might be really uncomfortable and not necessarily the path I want to take. Rather than all of that, why can't I just look at my "reaction" and decide to change it.

It's so easy to get bent out of shape over whether something or someone is right or wrong. As human beings we always want to categorize, label and put things in perspective. We require this framework for many different reasons; security, stability, a sense of normalcy, and a foundation to move forward from. The only difficulty lies in our inability to think differently or to exercise some flexibility in our thought patterns.

Once I have identified that I am at the source of my emotion I then get to choose if I want to justify how I'm feeling (be right about it) and continue feeling "angry" in this case or, perhaps I will choose to just "accept the situation as it is." He didn't keep his promise and I will choose not to have an emotional reaction to it. On further introspection, what I really want to know is why do I have so much emotional attachment to what another person says or does? What has that got to do with me and why am I so invested in it? While people often mirror myself back to me, they are also unique, separate individuals.

We are all on our own paths and sometimes those paths cross over, run parallel for a while and sometimes they then go on in different directions. During all of this WE GET TO CHOOSE OUR EMOTIONS. This choice gives you and me great power. I have the opportunity to change my experience of life through how I react to it.

*Moving Through Pain*

No person's life is completely free of pain. It is not my objective to lead a life free of pain. Rather, I want to be able to move through the pain, not stay stuck in it or feel immobilized both physically and emotionally. As an integral part of a healthy expression of who and what we are, it is essential that we are able to acknowledge to ourselves when we are experiencing pain. In the dark, quiet hours spent feeling our deepest emotions, we will also hear the small voice that tells us when it is time to pick ourselves back up and gently ease back into the lives we have.

What I have noticed in myself and others, is that when I am experiencing my pain, what is often the greatest balm is giving of myself and my talents to others. The simple act of service takes the attention off of me, which seems to offer the greatest reward. When I am focused on others, my pain lessens, I gain perspective and I get to be of value to others. Being of service acts like a tonic to my own emotional state.

Please hear that I am not trying to block out or not feel my pain, as I agree this would only worsen my own experience. There is no repression going on here. In fact, it is quite cathartic to hear of other people's experiences, trials and tribulations and to grieve with them in empathy. As I connect with my own pain, I take the opportunity to heal.

The Jungian concept of universal consciousness includes emotional and psychological pain. When I am truly connected to myself, and that includes even what I perceive to be as the unattractive parts, I become more connected to others. When I honour the beauty and what I may consider the less beautiful aspects of myself, I automatically give others permission to express themselves honestly. Suppression or repression of what is going on inside of me leads to a lack of integrity within myself. Other people pick up on this. It may not be what I'm saying or doing, but rather the lack of what I'm saying and doing. People feel this and know there is "something not quite right." This might lead to a lack of trust and respect. I will take those perceptions into myself. Again, all of this is usually not obvious or overt, but is rather happening on a subliminal level. That is why it is so critical to be completely honest at all times. If I am not honest with myself, how will I expect others to be honest with me?

People treat me how I treat myself, not only how I treat others. At any given time, I give people permission how to behave with me. I set the ground rules and also through my own behavior state how the "game" will be played. Moving through pain is just that "moving through it". It does not mean avoiding it, or dulling it through alcohol and drugs, but rather feeling the pain, and honoring and accepting the emotions and then allowing them their natural course of action. The use of the word "action" is very pointed as it relates to movement. When I am busy trying to analyze anything in my personal experience, I stop its natural movement. Our heads are very busy little computers, receiving, analyzing and storing data. If we just observe the data as it passes through, we lose our inclination to give it meaning. It's when we begin to have emotional attachments to the data that we allow ourselves to feel hurt, disappointed, distressed, frustrated or any other kind of negative emotion.

I think one of the most critical pieces of information I have ever received is, "Everything is neutral. Nothing has meaning, until I give it

48

meaning." If I had learned this as a teenager, I could have saved myself so much grief. Absolutely I give things meaning all the time. We are all judging and assessing machines. We want our lives to have meaning. What perverts the whole process of our lives is when we give things negative meaning and we feel pain as we think those thoughts.

As much as possible, when you are in the midst of experiencing emotional or psychological pain, say to yourself, "I feel _____." Fill in blank with the emotion you feel. Be honest with yourself and don't say, "Well I shouldn't be feeling that" or "I should be over that by now" or "I thought I had already dealt with that". Allow the experience, but don't get stuck in it.

When I bring awareness to whatever I am experiencing, I notice that the intensity of the emotion subsides and I begin to think as well as feel. However, one thing I have also noticed about myself is that I will behave in a manner that creates whatever juice or experience I am craving. For example, I know I am a master at creating drama when my life feels a little too level. I like excitement, passion and visceral experiences. I will seek to create drama, which gives me the charge I enjoy. I like my life to be intense. In my effort to experience intensity and passion, I occasionally operate in an unconscious manner. I may choose to create drama through misperceptions and misconceptions.

What I have to watch out for is my innate ability to create a truth from a perception. My beliefs become my truths, if I allow them to be. The key is realizing that at any given moment I GET TO CHOOSE MY ATTITUDE, OPINIONS FEELINGS AND RESPONSE. This is that master place again. I move from the robot to being in the driver's seat. It is so powerful and exceptional that the more I practice this concept, the more I incorporate it into my unconsciousness. This way I never feel victimized by my circumstances, but rather in I am in a position of power.

An exercise to try at this moment is this: Write down a situation when you experienced a huge surge of emotion, such as separation from a loved one, divorce, a child leaving home or even death. Write out all the emotions you felt in a paragraph form.

What I would like you to do now is write about the same situation but from the role of someone who knows you well, and is not expressing any of your emotions, but rather is stating the situation as it occurred. It could even be a newspaper reporter or T.V. broadcaster. They attempt to list the facts as they occurred subjectively and keep their opinions to a minimum.

Now I want you to read what you have just written aloud, but rather in the first person, as if you are the reporter and the person this happened to. Watch how your feelings shift as you are reading this aloud and then write about the feelings.

Again the idea here is not to discount your emotions, but rather to look at the situation that has brought these emotions up in you and look at them from a new perspective. The perspective that yes, the situation happened and I get to be at choice how I view it, think about it and feel about it. Also, I get to choose if I want to continue feeling that way and trust that it is in my best interest to do so. Most of all, don't block the emotions; allow them to flow through you in a natural manner and then most important of all, listen to the quiet voice that speaks to you at the end of the day. This is voice is your higher self, The Divine, and it will always guide you to what is the best for you.

### Feeding Passion

Before we discuss how to feed passion, we will get clear on the word "passion". Dictionary definition is: "strong feeling, the emotions as distinguished from reason; Rage, Anger; Love – also an object of affection or enthusiasm; sexual desire."

There is quite a dichotomy in the definitions. From love to rage, anger to sexual desire. No wonder this poor word is so often misunderstood during communications. I will be careful to make the distinction of which definition I am referring to when I use the word passion. In my section heading "Feeding Passion", I am referring to feeding love and strong feelings or intensity. How is that done, you wonder? Well, the key is first to discover your passion, your love. What do you have strong feelings about?

50

For me, I know I am passionate about communication, children, music, poetry, singing, art the welfare and well-being of the planet and healing of all living creatures. My personal experiences in healing were so profound that I feel it is my responsibility to share my newfound knowledge with as many people as possible. I now embrace my passion – my strong feelings of love – and share them with others. I no longer view passion as a word that masks only anger and rage.

Now that I know what I am passionate about, how do I feed it and why do I want to? The "why do I want to" part is easier for me to state. I want to feed my passions because during the experience of living passionately I feel more alive and joyful and more willing to contribute to others. Living the positive side of passion affects the endorphins in my brain – much the same as coffee and chocolate do, and I feel happier.

One thing that I want to stress is that the expression of passion may look different for everyone. Not everyone expresses passion loudly or vividly. It is very possible that the passion a person experiences is a very inner, deep, rich journey and they might appear peaceful and calm on the outside. Many people think the word passion only applies to artists and musicians and is closely synonymous to crazy. I believe that unbridled passion might look that way. However, as human beings, we are emotional creatures and avoiding feeling or expressing emotions may simply be a way of staying safe, especially if past experiences of passion were lived negatively. It is possible to experience and express passion as love and strong feelings in the most positive context possible. What is vital to consider is your intention or motivation in feeling and expressing what you say you want.

I know that if my intention is to communicate to another because I want to see them living in a happier and more peaceful way, and I am clear about this, my choice of words or expression are directed in this manner and are received much more openly by others. The feeding of my passion and love then becomes a two-way street. This is a beautiful and heart-moving experience to be in.

Many people relate to this feeling during the first bud of romance and falling in love. I would like to maintain that this experience might occur in *any* kind of relationship. It's all how we choose to feed the relationship. I might feed my relationships all kinds of poison such as jealousy, anger, resentment, rage, frustration or I might choose to feed my relationships love and life through kindness, patience, understanding and being open. I think the key is about being open. When I truly listen to others in an effort to understand them, rather than in an effort to prove myself right, I get the opportunity to learn and to be closer to that person and that ultimately feeds my desire to experience and express passion.

In essence the key to feeding passion is to first discover your passions. When you have done that, look at each one and uncover your motivation or what it is you want to experience Down the left-hand side of the page, write your passions. My list looks something like this:

Passions
Children
Music/Singing
Poetry
Art
Healing


When that is finished, go back to the beginning of your list and beside each passion write a few key words of what you want to experience.

| Passions | Key Words |
| --- | --- |
| Children | Joy, Playfulness, Curiosity |
| Music/Singing | Joy, Peace, Self-Expression |
| Poetry | Understanding, Connection, Self-Expression |
| Art | Expression, Communication |
| Healing | Intimacy, Connection |


Write out your list before proceeding to the next paragraph.

Now let's get back to the practical application of feeding our passions. If I am crystal clear about what it is I want to experience from each of my passions, then I line up my intentions and through congruency of intentions and actions, I move forward into actualization. Looking at my list of key words, I see some of the same words appearing - words such as intimacy, self-expression, connection and joy. These are critical ingredients to who I am and what I want out of life. I feed my passions by finding past-times, hobbies or activities that will give me the opportunity to experience these words, so even if I am not engaged in reading or writing poetry, I still experience understanding, connection and self-expression. The key words are really the essence of what I want to experience from my life, no matter what I am involved with.

## Chapter 6    CREATING THE IDEAL RELATIONSHIP

### Who Am I?

To the degree that I know myself and am happy with the relationship I have with me, will determine the degree that I am happy in relationship with others. Many times relationships with others are challenged to be successful because this question of "Who Am I?" is not fully understood. So, before going about creating the ideal relationship with another, let's take a serious look at your relationship with yourself. Quickly answer the following questions. For those that require a "yes" or "no", don't answer with a "sometimes" or "maybe".

The purpose of this exercise is to get clear, have fun and perhaps learn something you didn't know before. Some answers you may be unsure of so just skip that one and continue down the list. You may always come back to the ones you're not sure of and answer them last. There is no hidden agenda here or analytical summary based on how you answer the questions. This is information just for you, unless of course you choose to share it with others. That will be entirely your choice. Okay, here we go.

1.  Do you like yourself?
2.  Do you like to spend time by yourself?
3.  Would your best friend speak highly of you? What would they say?
4.  Do you love yourself?
5.  Have your parents or guardians given you a compliment in the recent past (or shortly before they died if they are no longer living)? Do you recall what that compliment was? If so, write it down here.
6.  What physical feature do you like the most about yourself?
7.  Do you like the sound of your voice on a tape or CD?
8.  Do you sing?
9.  Do you look people in the eye when you pass them on the street?
10. Do you smile at strangers?
11. Do you talk to strangers in an elevator or when waiting in line-ups?

12. Do you praise different parts of your anatomy?
13. Are you happy with your financial status?
14. Are you happy with your friends?
15. Are you happy with your parents?
16. Are you happy with your siblings?
17. Are you happy with your partner/spouse?
18. Are you happy with your children?
19. Are you happy with your job/career?
20. Are you happy with your health?
21. Are you happy right now?
22. Do you think you will be happy tomorrow?

After you have written out your answers to all of the above and any other comments that might be relevant, take a break from this book until tomorrow. It is very important to let all the information that is now in your consciousness to filter through your mind and feelings. Do not judge yourself. Simply observe what is going on and then let it go. Tomorrow or whenever you come back to this book will be the best time to continue on.

Okay, so now you're back. I wish I could hear from you what has been going on for you. I trust that the exercise above sparked some real deep thinking and contemplating of who you are. It will also be helpful to create your ideal relationship with yourself or at the very least, to understand what this means.

My ideal relationship with me is one that is free from worry, fear, and anxiety. I want to feel joyous, calm, inspired, peaceful and wise. I want to love what I see in the mirror everyday whether my eyes are puffy underneath, whether I've grown another wrinkle or gray hair or even if I have a huge pimple on my chin! I want to feel good inside no matter what is happening on the outside. For the most part this is true, but I'm human and I have moments where I don't' see the light at the end of the tunnel. How I realign myself is through reconnecting to the Divine, My passions, my relationships with others and my relationship with myself. When I look in the mirror and say, "Wow, you're very beautiful", or, "Gee, that colour really looks great on you!" I feel myself swelling up inside and feeling better. When I speak to myself in harsh tones or criticize myself, then the opposite occurs. I feel myself shrinking inside. Marianne Williamson was right when she said, "Your shrinking does not serve the world." This is true of you too.

We are all here for a purpose and developing a close, loving and intimate relationship with ourselves serves others. Knowing who you are and how you define your relationship with yourself is the very first step that you must take. That clarity will serve you when you begin relationships with other people. There are so many beautiful and inspiring books available to teach us about loving ourselves and loving others. I definitely recommend "The Inspiration" by Oriah Mountain Dreamer and The Mastery of Love by Don Miguel Ruiz, as a starting point.

### *Who is My Best Match?*

For decades people have turned to all kinds of sources outside of themselves to answer this question. This answer will definitely not be found in books, magazines, the internet or fortune tellers. Look inside yourself for this answer. You know with a deep and profound knowingness what you want from another. Rather than the traditional physical and material traits that we've been socially conditioned to look for in our mate, ask yourself, "What is the essence of what I want?"

At the age of 15 or so I wrote a poem about my soul mate. Try this exercise yourself and then don't be surprised when you actually manifest this person! Think about your characteristics when you are writing. Here is a sampling of what your letter or poem might look like.

"I create the perfect match for me. The person that best suits me intensely respects freedom of expression in others and in his or her self. He is kind and has infinite patience for other human beings. Harmony of spirit and harmony with all living creatures flows naturally from him. He is a passionate believer in equality, fairness and the right of every person to experience abundance on this earth. He is a passionate lover, tender father, loyal friend, and grateful son.

He is generous in spirit. The man best suited for me is a poet, artist, musician and philanthropist. He believes in sharing his talents and gifts with the world at large. He understands his purpose for being alive and relishes the concept that peace on earth is here and may be experienced by everyone. He thinks deeply, is slow to react and respond when attacked by others. He is willing to tread new paths and creates new avenues for people to express themselves. He is a consummate manifester and creates more than enough wealth for himself and anyone he feels responsible for. This person is unafraid of me and loves me enough that even when I'm angry, impatient and childlike, he won't leave me."

Now it is your turn to write your own menu, so to speak. Take your time. This is a vision that you are continuously creating whether you are single, married, or in any kind of relationship. What you are doing is creating your reality through your words. Be sure to revise any line that is not absolute truth for you. Your menu may be as long or as short as you want. It may be in bullet points, narrative, highly description or just a list of words. There is no right formula to writing out what it is you seek in your ideal partner. They key is to think about yourself rationally. Know what your weak points are and write down the complementary opposite of that, so you have it mirrored or modeled in the person you attract into your life.

What is most uncanny about this exercise is that even if you are in a relationship or marriage, this is an opportunity to get very clear about what is most important to you. Do not waste another moment being or doing what you don't want to do.

As well as including the essence of what you want in a partner, also include activities, hobbies, volunteer organizations that you are passionate about, and careers or vocations that have deep meaning for you. Once again, be as specific and detailed as possible. That is when the magic really starts to work. Begin writing out your list or poem now.

Now that you have written this out, don't file the piece of paper away where you will never find it again. Put in someplace where you will read it on a regular basis. Read it silently and read it aloud. If you have close friends that you feel comfortable and safe with, read it aloud to them. You may even want to put it to music. Wishes work best when they are put in a declaration format and are actually an "order" you are putting in to the universe; much like an "order" for a meal that a server puts in the kitchen. Now all you have to do is trust and wait and wait and trust.

### Where Do I Meet My Match?

Not surprisingly, many people think this is a key question. As a society, we have been conditioned to believe that anything we want, we must go out and search for. It's really very faulty thinking from a creative, magical, manifesting point of view. Looking outside of ourselves to satisfy what it is we want and crave usually leaves us feeling disappointed and disillusioned. The real test here is not to go to bizarre and unusual places to find our heart's desire. But then again, neither will lying around at home get you what you want.

The key is to first be very clear about what you want. Notice, that I did not say be clear about what you DON"T WANT. It will not serve you to focus on negatives. Be working on the positive. So, WHAT DO YOU WANT? When you've answered all of this based on the exercise above go about your normal life. Stay involved with people through school, work, volunteer activities, church, etc. The only thing that has changed before writing this exercise and now is you. You are more aware and conscious of what it is you want. Remain focused and clear about this as you talk to others, meet new people and perhaps see old friends and acquaintances in new ways.

Literally, what you are doing is changing the vibration around you. It is likely that people will begin seeing you differently as well. When any of us take our attention and focus off of the negative, or what it is we DON'T WANT or DON'T LIKE, we automatically set up a more positive vibration. Focusing on WHAT YOU WANT greatly assists the universe, God and others in answering you.

Always, always pay attention to the little voice inside of you. It will guide you when you are unsure of what to do in any given

58

situation. Many people believe the soft voice inside of you is your higher consciousness or the Divine speaking through you.

The "where" of meeting your soul mate or ideal partner is the least important part. Simply trust that the universe is unfolding as it should, and your requests or declarations will be delivered in the most opportune, divine timing. The where could be a place you go to on a regular basis such as the gas station, library, grocery store, etc. Keep your eyes, ears and heart open.

## *Getting Past The Mask – Mine and Theirs*

This is going to be a challenging section to write. First, I need to identify what a mask is so that as I use it throughout the next paragraphs we are clearly using the same definition.

The mask is an image I put up when I meet new people, or when I am uncomfortable, unsure of myself or afraid. It's the side of me that I refer to as my public self. She's pleasant, easy to talk to, non-confrontational, easy to be around.

In truth, when I'm feeling uncomfortable, unsure of myself or afraid, I'm anything but pleasant, easy to talk to, etc. But I use this mask of myself to hide behind as I gather myself together. This "mask" is what I want to be like, not necessarily what I'm really like.

Everyone wants to look good, be thought of well and remembered well. So, we pull out our masks because they are safe and they help us cope in situations when we are uncertain about being truly us – showing up as we truly are at any given moment. The problem is this – people only get to know each other's masks, not the true self.

It has been my experience that the more I focus on healing my pain and expressing my love, the more I am being who I truly am, rather that who I wish I was, which is the mask. When two people meet and they both put on their best faces, their "masks", what you have are two masks talking to each other. How then do people honestly assess and get to know each other and themselves when we live behind the "mask"? My answer is this, they don't. It is only when I am being truly myself without any concern another's reaction to me, that others know me.

Although this heading reads "Getting Past The Mask – Mine and Theirs", really, I am only in charge of myself, and getting past my own mask. As I drop my own mask, the other person is more likely to do the same thing. It is imperative that I know the difference between who I "think" I am and who I "truly" am. When I am consistently showing up in the world as who I truly am and how I'm honestly feeling at any given moment, I inadvertently give other people the opportunity to do the same. And that is the only influence I have on other people getting past their mask. The rest is up to them.

### *Accepting the Present*

Most of us are living our lives resisting our present (not unlike resisting a gift, as I realize the last word of my sentence could have more than one meaning.).

By resisting our present, I mean the present as in the now – this particular moment in time. Quite often I catch myself thinking well, once I have this or am doing that, *THEN AND ONLY THEN*, will I be happy. Partially it's the socialization and conditioning I've had until this moment, but it is also because there is something about my present moment that I am not enjoying. When I am not accepting my present, then I am not fully present in it. I am living in some other time frame, either the past or the future.

How do I fully accept the present when I am not happy with certain parts of my life? That is usually the question people find themselves asking. I believe it is a perfectly normal human condition to want to better ourselves and our life situations. We do this when we are seeking knowledge and education, more money, good jobs and rich relationships. The key is being happy along the journey. Once we fully appreciate and are grateful for what is occurring in this moment, we take the struggle out of the equation; the struggle between where we are right now and where we want to be. Ambition is a truly useful concept. It has helped the human race evolve to where we are now. Ambition lies steeped in possibility between the now and what might be. Where the strife usually occurs is when we see where we are and experience discontent. It is a short step to move from discontent into resistance.

The problem with thinking more about where we could be rather than where we are right now, is that truly all we really have is this particular moment in time. Our only real ability lies in fully comprehending and acting in this moment. The rest of life (past and future) are fantasies. They're not real. Only this moment in time is real. We plan for the future, but the living occurs now.

If you think you will be happy only once you have created a large, lush English garden, but you don't have the money or means to do it, find out what experience you are looking to accomplish and think how you might create the experience in other ways.

I used to think I could only write once I owned my own home with a study or office. This study had to have large windows looking out on the ocean with a huge strip of white sandy beach. The experience I was looking for was inspired solitude, peace and calmness. Well, I am currently writing this book while sitting on my bed looking out a window onto giant oak trees. I have a lovely hanging basket full of petunias right outside the window and am in a quiet neighbourhood. I've structured my work schedule so that I am home on Wednesday afternoons while my son is still in school. I've created the solitude I wanted as well as the quiet, peace and calm. I didn't need to own my own home or have my own office or study. Most importantly I stopped resisting the present as it exists and focused on how I would create what I wanted, which was the physical and mental place to do my writing.

The same is true of money and relationships. Once we are really clear about what we want and we commit to it, we may choose to move into action to begin creating whatever it is we want. In the present moment, however, it is important to fully appreciate that which we do have. I know that when I am focused on all the attributes I really love about my husband, I behave more lovingly towards him, which in turn leads to me experiencing more love in my life.

I have also made some shifts to have what I want as far as my finances. I created a raise for myself at work and also looked at all the money I was paying out to see what could be eliminated. Critical to this process was that during all of this I remained truly grateful and appreciative of the abundance I was currently experiencing. This mind-set allowed me to move from resisting what already existed in my life, to accepting life in the present moment.

Take a look at your present life, not that which you had or want to have, but exactly where you are right now. As a writing exercise, the following will be even more deeply ingrained into your consciousness and may be used for reprogramming yourself into living more deeply in the present.

Write down these headings.

1.  Vocational Life (Work, School or What I do with the Majority of My Time)
2.  Financial Life
3.  Spiritual or Religious Life
4.  Love Life

Beginning with number one - Vocational Life - write out what that is for you right now. Use as many descriptive and emotional words as possible. It is critical that you stay with the present. Do not write about the past or the future, but stay with how that part of your life is currently. When you are completely finished writing about this area of your life, move on to number two and do the same thing. Write about your current Financial Life in great detail. Then do the same for numbers three and four.

After you have completed this writing exercise, read through what you have written, paying special attention to the tone of the words. Have you written about what you are grateful for or what you think is lacking? Did you stay focused in the present? Did you write about your life in a factual or emotional way? If you have not written about anything that you are grateful about, notice this and be curious about why that is. Think if there is anything you might add to this area of your life that you are grateful for and write it down as well.

Conversely, if you have written quite a bit about what is lacking in your life, notice that and be curious about yourself and how this came to be. Think about some tiny, baby steps you could make to turn your situation around.

Don't judge or criticize yourself for any thoughts you may have, simply write down the suggestions for improving that area of your life and reflect upon them later.

All of these exercises are for your own personal use only. At no point, am I going to suggest you publish your writings or share with other people. Only do so if you really want to.

This entire book is about the journey and discovery of yourself. Here is an opportunity to develop a closer relationship with you that will aid you to move from feeling pain to experiencing passion and peace.

## Chapter 7    *PUTTING PASSION INTO PARTNERSHIPS*

### *Where is the Fire?*

Are you currently in an intimate love relationship? If you are not in an intimate love relationship and do not wish to be this chapter will not apply to you. However, if you are not in a relationship and would like to be, I want you to think about this chapter from the perspective of the ideal relationship you would like to have and apply the following concepts to it. Before we proceed, I would like to add an excerpt taken from a magazine called Eagle Eye, April-May-June 2004 edition. The title of the article is "The Longing for LOVE is a Spiritual Call". The quote is as follows,

"People who are not in a relationship close themselves down out of fear of being hurt or fear of not finding the 'right one'. People who are in relationships find thousands of ways to turn away, to keep distance between themselves and others, to be critical or irritated or whatever it takes. This is all ego fighting to keep itself alive. Ego wants to keep you believing that fear is more powerful and that Love will hurt you. Once you understand the truth, the big picture, you will understand just how absurd this is. Love is your highest truth, the essence of your being, your connection with Me (me being the Divine or God)."

This excerpt spoke so deeply to me for a variety of reasons. First I thought of all my single friends – those who are single through divorce and those who are single and have never married. I then thought about my own marriage – twenty-six years worth and I saw how the comment of keeping distance was so true with respect to my attitudes over parts of my marriage. I allowed my fear and my ego to run the show. Fear of being hurt, fear of being wrong, fear of losing myself, fear of having made a mistake – the list goes on and on. My ego, what I term my small ego is that part of me that is not interested in the grand scheme of life and Spirit, but is only concerned with being right, being superior and all the really small, petty, unpleasant parts of who I am. I know they are there and serve a purpose. The key is to not let my small ego run my life. My large Ego is the ego connected to Spirit, Life, God/Goddess the Divine Source and Energy. When my large Ego is active, I operate without fear. I lose my concern to be right and become less critical and irritated.

The heading "Where Is the Fire?" speaks directly to my connection with Spirit and my large Ego. The fire is the passion, the source of life that everyone wants to be plugged into! It's the part of us that loves to celebrate, to feel excitement, energy and enthusiasm. It's the reason we fall in love, party, play sports, participate or look at art, participate or listen to music. It is the joie de vivre! The joy of life and living!

Without that spark, that fire, we may feel dead inside. It is possible that life may seem pointless and our purpose here a slow, meandering without direction or reason. In our relationships this is critical. When we welcome relationships into our lives, we feel more alive. Yes, on our own we often feel safer, more secure and less afraid, yet we also rob ourselves of the pleasure and intensity and rich rewards of being in relationship with others. It is possible to feel safe, secure and courageous in relationship with others. Yes, all of these qualities and more are what I experience inside my relationship.

### How To Find the Magic

If you are in a current relationship and are wondering where is the passion, think back to when you first met each other. What was the spark? Did you share common interests that you no longer pursue? Was it an exciting, physically adventurous relationship with a lot of sports and physical activities? Was it a relationship of long walks on the beach, sitting in a front of a fire, listening to music, watching old movies, reading, writing or talking long into the night? Try to recall when you first fell in love. What was the attraction?

It is essential to retain the elements that first drew you together. Make spending time together a priority. Find the time and put it on the top of your "To Do List". It's amazing how many couples say they "just don't have the time". Time has not changed. The only thing that has changed is what you are doing with your time!

Don't miss this point. Your relationship is only as good as the time, energy and effort you invest into it. Don't blame the other person. If you're unhappy, take the initiative to make things better.

Perhaps it is as simple as making love more often. Sex is a great stress reliever. It helps put all the day-to-day problems into perspective. It also unites people in more than a physical way. It gives you the opportunity to deal with life together, to become united mentally and spiritually.

If you have issues around sex that you have been holding on to due to past hurts, it is time to seek the counsel of a sex therapist or psychologist. Don't waste another moment not enjoying this great gift we have as human beings to experience joy, pleasure and ultimate physical satisfaction.

If you are not currently in a relationship, consider what is most important to you in a partner and not just the physical attributes, but what kind of experiences or emotions you want to have with a partner. Consider what is juicy and rewarding to you. What really constitutes a full, rich experience of life? It is the essence of relating to another human being that most of us want, not the package that people come in. What are you passionate about? What activity do you absolutely want to share with another individual? It's the things that are of vital importance to us that matter in long run. So consider all of these things, when you ask yourself why there are no passionate relationships in your life, or why your current relationship is lacking fire and passion. Begin writing out the answers to the questions above now.

## *What To Do with Anger*

Western and European societies have conditioned people at an early age into believing that anger is an unhealthy emotion and that we should avoid expressing anger.

For example, Zeno (333 BC - 264 BC) of Citium was one of the first Europeans to struggle with the relationship between the mental and emotional realms that represent the two fundamental capacities of human existence: knowing and loving. Zeno's teachings have been passed on, including his main concept that "tranquility can best be reached through indifference to pleasure and pain". Many Europeans adopted this philosophy and passed it on through the centuries, believing that emotions had no value and were better off suppressed and unexpressed.

A long time ago a young man told me he thought it was highly inappropriate to express anger. I remember how passionately I defended my right to express anger. Anger is such a strong and powerful emotion that burying it inside of ourselves, and not allowing it expression tends to have extremely detrimental effects on our physical, mental and emotional bodies. I believe even to the point of creating cancer, heart attacks and other fatal diseases.

Since I maintain that the expression of anger is a healthy, normal part of being a human being, you're probably wondering how, where and when do we express anger that does not hurt ourselves or others? Good question.

The answer is that we must always speak our truth... but with compassion. We maintain being centered and calm if we lose our attachment to our belief systems. Anger stems from holding onto belief systems and believing that being right is more important than getting along with others or accomplishing team goals. When we feel taken advantage of, hurt, abused or find ourselves in any other kind of victim situation we tend to react with anger. Focus on remembering that no matter what occurs in your life you are in charge of your reaction to it. At any given time as an adult I choose what is happening in my life and I also get to choose my reaction to it.

If I remember that everything is neutral and nothing has meaning until I give it meaning, then I free myself up to be detached from what others think, say or do. If I am not seeking approval from others (which tends to be a huge trap anyways), it does not matter so much if others don't agree with me or blatantly disagree with me. I have space in my mind and heart to allow for the differences and say, "That's fine. It doesn't really matter that we don't agree 100 percent. Where do we go from here?"

If I am willing to stop taking other people's thoughts and ideas about me PERSONALLY, then I will really focus on what is important. Is action needed? Is there a joint effort that requires compromise and team work? Will I let go of my need to be right and move forward into "Right (Higher Ego) Action" instead? By addressing these questions I focus less on anger and more on enjoying the passion and peace that I want to experience in my relationships.

Next, we will look at how peace enters the equation as far as close personal relationships are concerned.

The following is a quote taken from a newsletter I receive from Elyse Killoran and in it she has taken an excerpt from Marianne Williamson's book, "A Return to Love: Reflections on the Principles of A Course in Miracles". I believe the following information speaks directly to the role emotions plays in our relationships and also speaks directly to our taking responsibility for our own emotions.

## CREATING PEACE

"You'll know that you are Deliberately Creating Peace when... you notice that, when someone 'pushes your buttons', instead of expending your energy trying to get the other person to change, you search inside yourself and ask, 'what happened inside me that led me to react that way to you?' Whenever we feel a painful emotion (anger, resentment, jealousy, fear, depression, desire for vengeance, grief) this simply means that someone has activated one of our wounds and a powerful opportunity for healing is right in front of us.

The next time you find that your 'buttons' have been pushed where will you focus your attention -- inward or outward?
Recognize that your point of power lies within (Tuning In):
The shift from fear to love is a miracle. It doesn't fix things on the earth plane; it addresses the real source of our problems, which is always on the level of consciousness. Love in your mind produces love in your life. This is the meaning of Heaven. Fear in your mind produces fear in your life. This is the meaning of hell.

A shift in how we think about life produces a shift in how we experience it. The return to love is the great cosmic drama, the personal journey from pretense to self, from pain to inner peace.

68

When we love, we are automatically placing ourselves within an attitudinal and behavioral context that leads to the unfolding of events at the highest level of good for everyone involved. We don't always know what that unfoldment will look like, but we don't need to."

Marianne Williamson, "A Return to Love: Reflections on the Principles of A Course in Miracles"

## *Why is Passion Underrated?*

The word passion brings up all kinds of images or more specifically, all DIFFERENT kinds of images for different kinds of people. In chapter four, I gave the dictionary definitions of passion. For years, the word passion, held only the meaning of the darker emotions, those emotions which caused pain. So of course, being a person who wanted to experience only the positive side of life, I discounted the word passion as something that was not for me. I did not embrace the word as something I wanted to have as a part of my life. I did not want to take on the energy of passion or wear it any sense of the word. It was dark and unpleasant. I gave the word "passion" no beneficial value whatsoever.

In parts of Europe (from which many people in North American have emigrated or descended from), the word passion held a connotation of rebellion, uprising, insurgence and everything that the "Catholic Church" held in disdain. So, of course, passion was discouraged in all of its forms. It was better that people be as even-tempered and even-natured as possible. Strong emotion of any kind was not well tolerated, even to the point of laws being developed around "appropriate public behavior". For centuries, we have been conditioned to believe that the more neutral we were in temperament and communication the more accepted we would be.

Luckily, North America and Europe do not represent the entire world population, for there are many countries whose culture embraces passion and strong emotion. These countries do not try to contain passion and relegate it only for actors, musicians and others who have chosen the field of "entertainment". Rather these cultures have accepted the diversity of emotions that reside in each human being.

The word acceptance is key here. Being open and accepting of others, and especially of ourselves, lowers our rejection and resistance and in turn, our struggle with life.

The positive side of passion is its depth and intensity. Living passionately is an opportunity to experience great joy, humour, laughter and happiness.

Now let's look at the word passion in context of our most important intimate and personal relationships. Passion is an opportunity to communicate with others on an honest and deep level. When we express ourselves passionately, it assists us in stating either verbally or non-verbally what is most important to us, what is of the greatest value and what we care most deeply about.

We all know how music affects our emotions, yet we are reluctant to allow these same emotions to be displayed in our verbal and non-verbal communications. Somehow the display of strong emotions has created fear and security issues within us. We don't feel safe when others are expressing themselves strongly. We go into resistance or try to pacify the other person so that we have some safety parameters and then deal with life in a more "reasonable and logical" fashion. It is this striving towards logic, reason and safety occasionally makes us feel crazy. The world and the people living in the world are not always reasonable, logical. Remember the chaos theory? From chaos eventually emerges order.

It is during the process of allowing of chaos in our lives that we move forward and experience all of life deeply, richly and in a way that is ultimately the most satisfying and rewarding.

### Passion and Peace United

When you read these words together, did you right away think, "Well, they don't belong together; that's kind of like mixing oil and water"?

Well, perhaps at first glance it does seem a bit ironic that passion and peace are concepts that could be united, but quite honestly it all comes down to intent. When I am feeling deeply and passionately about something and I want to express that emotion, what is my intent behind expressing the emotion? Do I want to feel closer to that person and, be as in sync as possible? Or do I want them to move away from me, create distance and discord? The first thing we need to do is examine whether we are expressing passion in a negative or positive sense. Obviously, passion expressed negatively will create more distance between two people. And conversely, the opposite will be true. The more positively I am expressing passion, the more others will be drawn to me.

It is possible for life to be intense, rich and rewarding. My passion is my sense of how deeply I am experiencing any and all aspects of my life. Living life without emotion or intensity leaves me feeling flat and I do not equate that feeling with being calm or at peace. Rather it is when my experience of life is deep and passionate that I feel most at peace.

It's important to note that although this book is being written in English, everyone who speaks English may give different words different meanings.

The intent behind my writing this book is my attempt at uniting people in a common understanding to move forward from a feeling of unease or pain to a feeling of passion and ultimately peace.

At the heart of this understanding is the comprehension of our beauty, perfection and Godliness. Each time we reject ourselves or others, we are rejecting the Divine. This creates our sense of distance, detachment, loneliness and depression. We are connected not just spiritually or by scientific classification, but also our physicality is connected with every other molecule and atom within our universe.

I sincerely believe that when passion is defined and expressed in a manner that creates unity, true inner and outer peace is achieved.

## Chapter 8      THE WORLD'S SECRET TREASURE

### Saving and Celebrating Our Children

So much has been researched, discussed and written about children. One of the key things I believe we are missing about our children is that they are in fact people. Albeit smaller than adults, they experience life with the same intensity as we do. They have thoughts, feelings, considerations, fears and the whole gamut of emotions. When I came up with the heading "Saving Our Children", there was so much to consider. People spend considerable time and money on the protection and preservation of our environment. Yet what if we gave just as much, if not more time, energy and money to the protection and preservation of children? Not just the children of the rich and famous or even the wealthy western children, but all children around the globe. What if we really grasped the concept that children today are the investment in the preservation of the human race? Do you think you would behave differently towards any child that you encountered? Would you take more time to be considerate, kind and respectful?

I have a son who at the time of writing this section is 14 years old. Every day I see him changing from a boy to a young man. With him I have the opportunity to express patience instead of irritation, kindness instead of aggravation, love in place of manipulation and deceit.

It is so important for all of us to examine our relationship with children. Do we inadvertently or unconsciously treat them as second-class citizens; for some reason less worthy of our courtesy and respect? And if we are doing that, why are we doing that?

Many of us have learned our parental attitudes from our parents and for the most part never questioned those attitudes. Now is the ideal time to look at this, for it bears heavily on the future of how our children will be as they become adults.

If every time you thought of this fact, "How I speak to a child directly impacts and will likely be emulated and mirrored by this child in his/her relationships with others", would you change your treatment of children? It is a responsibility to be a parent or parental figure in a child's life. It is also a huge opportunity to play a pivotal role.

Many children live in a home with parents who largely live unconsciously. Moving from day to day they do the best that they know how and spend more time working to put food on the table and a roof over their children's head, than considering how their words and actions are impacting the lives of their children and not only the child's present life, but also their future lives.

All words uttered and actions taken have an immediate impact on the psyche of others within our field of existence. What I put out to the world is almost instantly manifested back to me. If I believe in the goodness of the universe then that is my experience of the universe. The same is true of children. If I believe they are generally brats, all my experiences of children will reflect bratty behaviour that just further supports my initial belief. And that is the big challenge! To change our beliefs, thoughts and feelings will have momentous and instantaneous repercussions.

If we begin to view our children as ourselves, we also have the chance to heal the pain and suffering experienced in our own young lives, which in turn directly affects who we are now as adults.

Children respond to love and energy. The bigger our energy that is packed with fun and excitement, quite often the more children respond to us. They came into this life knowing what makes them feel good. Love expressed in a way that makes a child feel safe is the surest way to ensure that child grows up feeling confident and prepared for any adversity.

Conversely a child who experience negative forms of energy, such as abuse, neglect, fear and trauma, grow up fearful, non-confident, angry, sad and depressed. The saddest part is quite often the form of energy they experienced from their parents is what they continue to seek out when they become adults. The phrase negative attention is better than no attention has been bandied about for decades.

The truth is children do thrive under attention. They grow up physically, emotionally and mentally under the influences they experience in their environment, through parents, teachers, their peers, their church, and extra curricular activities. If you are a parent or have the role of a parent, how is your child spending their time? What kind of attention are they receiving from others including yourself?

If you are a parent, guardian or experience children in your life, what kind of energy do you believe these children are experiencing? Take some time to write out your answers to this question.

As adults we are products of our own childhood. After having completed the exercise above, if it was applicable to you, now is the time to list how you would have liked to be treated as a child. What are some characteristics that you think would have aided you as you grew up, moving from childhood to adolescence to adult hood? List those characteristics now.

What I would you to do now is look at this list and beside each characteristic, write a "yes" if you believe you possess that characteristic now and write a "no" if you believe you don't. Consider the "no's" and ask yourself why you don't possess those characteristics. Take some time to reflect on it, then write a few paragraphs about any insights you may have.

I would like you to look at your initial list of characteristics and now beside all of those which you had written a "yes", determine if you treat your children or the children that you know with these same characteristics. Again, for all of those that you say "no" to, take some time and ponder why you don't. Then write a few paragraphs on any insights that came up for you.

The previous exercises were designed to help you make the direct connection between the person you are today, the child you were and how you treat children in your life. We cannot positively impact children until we understand what it is that we offer them.

The opportunity to positively impact a child today, gives us a chance to heal our own wounds that we suffered as children. The more we heal all of our very old wounds, the quicker we accelerate on our path of healing and living our true potential as adults.

## *The Animal Kingdom*

In our journey from pain to passion, I would like you to consider the role of animals in our lives.

I believe there is a direct connection from passion to peace and that animals have a natural way of living that we might learn from if we take the time to think and study about the following ideas.

Have you ever been curious about why we share this planet with animals? For those of us who are not vegetarian or vegan, one of our first responses might be that animals are here as an edible source of protein. Isn't it odd to think that over the ages, the human race has made determinations over which animals to domesticate, which animals are holy, which animals to eat and which animals remain wild? What is also very interesting is that these criteria change from continent to continent and country to county.

If animals were not a source of food, what other reason would there be for them to be on the planet?

Scientists have uncovered many mysteries surrounding the age of dinosaurs and how our current breeds of mammals, animals and reptiles have evolved from those creatures of long ago. What has not been explained clearly, well at least to me, is why certain creatures died out, yet others have not.

Our planet is so rich and diverse, not only in plant life, but also in the animal kingdom. Some of the animals naturally prey upon a select group of other animals. There is a complete and delicate eco system balance at work that is a marvel to learn about.

We have heard time and time again, that man's blundering and destruction of forests, jungles and natural habitats upset this eco system.

Also, how was it ever determined which animals were suitable for hunting? There was a time when game was hunted for survival. Now we are educated enough to know that there are other forms of plant life that will adequately serve our need for protein. Yet it has also been proven that plants are alive, yet the vegetarians and vegans never seem to acknowledge this fact when disputing the eating of animals.

Regardless of how we evolved and determined which animals and plants to eat in order to sustain our race, there is still a valuable role that animals play in the lives of humans.

Our domesticated creatures become a part of our families, our homes and our hearts. Who hasn't seen the little dog in a sweater or knit coat? People are carrying their animals in what were previously described only as baby carriers. Does this speak to our innate need to nurture? Even for childless people, there often appears to be the need to care for others, whether people or animals.

Domestic animals reward our attention to them with cuddling, quiet, soft murmurings or sounds and a soft, furry coat that we like to stroke and scratch. What is this relationship all about? I believe that people have established relationships with animals for a multitude of reasons. Many people are find it too challenging to be with people due to pain and challenges they experienced early in their lives. Animals are generally easier to be around. They have their basic needs, and when those are met are often very pleasant to be around.

Some researchers have determined that animals aid in the healing process of seniors and children. Some hospitals have included wards for pets to be brought in so the animals are available to be accessed by their patients. How amazing is this?

Dogs have been trained for blind people. An important role, don't you think? While we have many reasons for loving and caring for our domestic pets, why are we not as generous with animals in the wild?

It appears that all creatures have a role and purpose for being here. Is it such a stretch to believe we might all live on this planet together harmoniously? These are ideas to consider and write about before continuing to the next subject heading. Think about how animals might assist you and others in healing pain, both physical and emotional. Include ideas about this in your writing exercise.

## Ruling the World as Stewards

I've included a chapter on this subject because as we heal ourselves internally, our focus naturally turns to our external environment. The planet is also in need of healing. Becoming more focused on our home, our planet is becoming more and more mainstream thinking. Like anything, I look for a motivating reason to participate beyond my own private world and become involved in global movements. I trust the following will resonate with you as well.

Two of the words in this subheading speak very loudly to me. The first is the word "ruling" and the second word is "steward". Let's examine the words one by one before proceeding into the subject matter in more detail. Going back to the dictionary, let's look at the definition of each word.

### Ruling/Rule *(noun)*
1. *A guide or principle for governing action: REGULATION;*
2. *The usual way of dealing with something;*
3. *The exercise of authority or control: GOVERNMENT;*

### Ruler - Rule *(verb)*
1. *CONTROL: also: GOVERN;*
2. *To be supreme or outstanding in;*
3. *To give or state as a considered decision*

### Steward *(noun)*
1. *One employed on a large estate to manage domestic concerns;*
2. *One who supervises the provision and distribution of food (as on a ship); also: an employee on a ship or airplane who serves passengers;*
3. *One actively concerned with the direction of the affairs of an organization.*

Now you might possibly begin to understand my excitement about this subject. When I wrote the heading I was thinking of the word "ruling" as "the exercise of authority or control" or "to govern".

While the bible speaks of humans as having rulership and dominion over the planet, I believe that the Great Divine intended us to rule with wisdom, foresight, kindness and consideration. Even if your beliefs do not encompass what is in the bible, it is in fact an immense responsibility to have rulership over this planet.

As stewards or caretakers of the planet it makes sense that we want to be informed of what's going on with our home. We are here now and it is in our everyday moments that we may choose to be conscious of our thoughts, words and actions and how they are impacting not only the people around us, but also the planet at large. The use of pesticides, aerosol cans, toxic foods, etc., all affect our planet adversely. If we choose responsibly we choose to change our behaviors. After all, when we leave, we are bequeathing the planet to the following generations. What chance will they have for survival and fruition if their home is no longer tenable?

Having this planet is a gift. There is so much beauty and wonder on it. The earth sustains us, nurtures us, protects us and provides for all that we need. It's a wonderful home, especially when you consider our known alternatives; living in space, or on an inhospitable planet in the solar system that we know. All food would have to be manufactured. Most likely we will not have lakes and oceans to swim in or fresh air to breathe or the beauty and magnificence of the seasons to experience. Imagine never seeing the full spectrum of colours in autumn or walking in the rain or snow, not ever breathing in the sweet scent of spring, or the crisp, clean mountain air. Imagine living in a cold austere environment where likely everything is moderate or kept the same; same temperature, same air control, same weather.

It is easy to forget what we have or to take it for granted as always being available to us and our heirs, however if we continue on our destructive path, the earth will no longer be available to us.

As stewards, it's worthwhile to make sure we are in alignment with protecting and fostering the earth so that it continues its existence in the centuries and millennium to come.

If you believe that we experience many lifetimes, don't you want to ensure that we have a planet to come home to? I know I do. It's in my best interests to protect the planet for everyone.

Coming back to the title of this book, "From Pain to Passion – the Journey of Self-healing", I believe that thoughtful and considered stewardship of this planet is also about healing. As any kind of healing takes place, whether on the individual level, group level, animal level or planet level – we are affecting the healing of the whole. We are so intricately interconnected with all that is in our physical universe, that our presence affects all that is around us.

We are connected in this way. I'm sitting on a chair that is connected to the floor, which is connected to my house that is connected to the earth that is connected to wherever you are. This is how you and I are connected on the physical level. We also breathe the same air that surrounds our planet, look at the same sky (albeit a different section of the sky), see the same moon, stars and sun and on and on we go. This explains our physical connection.

Following the premise that thoughts, feelings, words and action are all energy, it is reasonable to assume that all of these are connected to an outer field of energy, not just our own internal energy. If this concept is a stretch for you, consider the following. Have you ever had the experience of thinking something just to have someone that you are with speak it aloud milliseconds later? Or have you ever felt a certain way, expressed that feeling to another just to hear that they feel the same way? The same might be said of words and actions. Quite often we attract to ourselves people who are of a similar nature. This is what I refer to as a "field of energy". I believe that as a race we traverse the earth in groups of like-minded individuals, whether it is a shared culture, race, religion, socio-economic background, etc. What we share is not as critical as the fact that we are sharing an energy field.

A large part of the energy field is affected by sound. And since sound is what I create when I speak or sing, I am affecting the energy field with my voice. I believe that what Don Miguel Ruiz says about "Being impeccable with my word" is critical and essential to the reality I want to create. My word is my voice, whether that word is spoken or written. Time and time again, life has proven to me that my results are in direct relation to my voice.

When considering the planet and the concepts of healing, is it not critical that you and I are constantly in touch and conscious of what we're saying and doing so that we are in alignment with the healing that we want to achieve?

I know I want people around me who want to move forward in a constructive and enlightened fashion using their consciousness to improve themselves and the world around them. For the most part I have achieved this.

In closing, the same is true with respect to the stewardship of this planet that we call earth. If we use our consciousness in a constructive manner, and come from an intention of wanting to impact the world around us in a positive manner, then it naturally follows that our thoughts, feelings, words and actions will all be congruent and will in fact affect the people and the planet at large in a positive and constructive manner.

## *My Responsibility*

You will notice that the above heading uses the word "My", not "Your" and the reasoning for this is simple. I am only responsible for myself, so this section of the book is going to be about how "my responsibility" fits into the theme of my journey of self-healing.

There is one other reason that this chapter heading is here too and that is to check out for yourself while you are reading it, to see if you want to adopt any of the concepts for yourself. All of the previous chapters may have alluded to this concept to varying degrees, but here we are going to explore it in more depth.

Looking at the word responsibility as my ability to respond, I get the sense that I am in the driver's seat. At any and all times, it is my choice and I emphasize the word CHOICE, to respond. Not only is it my choice to respond, but I also get to choose HOW I want to respond to people, situations or any set of circumstances. A point of fact for me is that I know I am able to respond, yet the key is to not go into "an automatic response" or what I term "the automan or robot". The robot is the part of me that responds to people and situations in the way that I always have without thinking or considering the implications of my actions. This manner of responding could be something I learned early in life or it could be something I've emulated from my parents, teachers, siblings, etc.

It is not as essential to know where I learned these responses, but more importantly to know clearly what these responses are and whether or not they are serving me. It is likely you have heard or even use the term "serving" before. In the event that you have not, consider it to be how well any kind of response is working for you in a way that you like. Are the direct results of your responses results that you enjoy? If my responses and results are not serving me, it is likely I need to take a look at my responses and see what I might change so that my outcomes are more favorable.

Now you will likely have noticed, since you are all intelligent people (or you wouldn't have been attracted to my book-yes I'm complimenting you and me at the same time!), that in the above paragraph, I'm keeping the focus and the "responsibility" on myself. I truly believe that each of us "attracts to us that which occurs", a term borrowed from Context Associated. Following this philosophy, whatever is occurring in my life is in direct relation to how I am and how I respond. This is actually an excellent theory! Excellent because it affords me the opportunity to change whatever I don't like and not to feel like I am victimized or at the mercy of whatever is occurring.

Another essential element to consider when thinking about my results and my responses is whether or not I am behaving consciously or unconsciously. When I am being the robot I am unconscious and simply thinking and behaving in the way that I always do without being entirely present. I slip into my "automatic" behavior as quickly and easily as my favorite flannel pajamas.

When I am being conscious and present in my life, everything becomes focused. My thoughts, feelings words and actions become very deliberate. Imagine! I actually consider what I am going to say rather than just speaking it! Very challenging for someone who loves talking!!

As a conscious thinking person I generally accept more readily the results in my life and own the fact that I am responsible for them. It is only when I behave or think from an unconscious perspective that I generally dislike my results and then don't easily fathom how the results came to be.

Everything and I mean literally everything in my life is of my creation! The same is true for you. As you're reading this take a look around you, I mean literally take a look at your physical environment. Are you able to determine how the items that surround you came to be in your life? Most likely you can. It is the intangible results that are the most difficult to assess how they came to be. For example, how did you attract your most intimate partner or conversely, how did you attract a lack of a partner. Was it conscious or unconscious?

Do you know precisely what characteristics or traits you like about your partner or for that matter, even the traits you appreciate the most in your friends? Do you recall the exact moment you said "Yes", I want this person in my life or "No", I don't want an intimate partner or any close friends in my life. If you are able to honestly say "Yes", I remember it all and I specifically state what, when, how and why I attracted these people or attracted a lack of people into my life, you are indeed a rare individual. Most of us are able to recall many of the results in our life, but generally not everything.

Another difficult and sometimes mysterious result to figure out is our level of finances. Are you happy with your financial situation? If not, why is it this way? And in answering, will you do so without blaming another person or set of circumstances? What feelings, thoughts or beliefs do you have that have predetermined your level of finances?

If I honestly believe that I attract to me that which occurs, this means I am also responsible for the level of financial wealth that I am currently experiencing. This may be a sobering thought for people.

Use this time to write down all of your thoughts around your financial status. Do you have enough money? Do you have lots of money? Whose ideas around money have you adopted? What were their attitudes towards money? Begin writing out these thoughts now.

Now take as much time as necessary to do the same writing experience but do it for your most intimate relationship or lack of relationships. For example, is your current most intimate relationship or lack of relationship satisfying to you? Do you have enough intimacy in your life? Whose attitudes and ideas around relationships have you adopted? What was their attitude towards relationships? Write down your thoughts now.

## *Raising Awareness*

This section will be about how we may raise our awareness so that we are operating more from our conscious selves and less from our unconscious. This is turn is going to have a very positive and beneficial outcome on all aspects of our lives. It has been my experience that once I begin focusing on improving one area of my life, say my marriage, it has a direct impact on all other areas at the same time.

Now the big question, how does one go about raising their awareness? Well, to begin with there has to be an honest desire to want to increase your awareness. If you feel you have this, you have passed the first hurdle.

By having the intention of increasing awareness in your mind, you may begin to feel somewhat vulnerable initially because you are going to want to solicit feedback from people around you. The best place to start with increasing awareness is to look in the mirror and begin with you. Many people have found that prayer and meditation increases their level of self-awareness. If neither of these principles appeals to you, then I suggest that you be willing to spend at least half an hour a day in silence. Silence means you cut yourself off from any external stimuli; no music, television, phones, email, internet, etc.

Find a comfortable place in your home where you truly relax and experience quietness. You may want to have pen and paper or a journal nearby as many people have random thoughts running through their mind when they first begin this technique. The following is a process to follow once you have decided to undertake being in silence for at least half an hour per day.

1. Sit or lie down in your comfortable place. Make certain you are not wearing uncomfortable clothing or jewellery.

2. Take ten deep breaths, breathing in through your nose and out through your mouth. With each breath, feel your body relaxing more and more. Focus on relaxing each part of your body beginning with your feet and moving all the way up. Tell your body to relax by saying, "I relax my feet. My feet are relaxed. I relax my ankles. My ankles are relaxed." Continue with these words until you have spoken to all parts of your body.

3. As you are relaxing, observe the thoughts that are going through your mind. If you find that a particular thought or series of thoughts continues in a circular fashion (meaning it comes, goes and then returns), open your eyes, write the thought down and then repeat #2 until your entire body is relaxed.

If you fall asleep, that is a normal reaction and don't worry about it. The more you practice this method, the more likely you will remain conscious. What is really important is to review any circular thoughts you may have. This is where the greatest percentage of your conscious mind is focused on. If they are items beyond your control and may take place in the future, you need to tell your mind that you will deal with these items later by stating the time and date you will deal with them.

Part of increasing awareness is to reeducate and reprogram your mind so that it is functioning to its best capacity and working in a way that assists you.

Many people don't realize that our minds are containers for all that we have experienced to date. All of the data that we have heard, seen and observed gets filtered through our experiences and stored in the mind. Many of our fears are learned behaviours that we picked up unconsciously from other people. It requires a great deal of discipline to unlearn these thoughts and reformat them in a way that serves us more efficiently.

If you have concerns about an intimate relationship with a specific person, write down those concerns and then ask the person's permission to speak with them about these thoughts. Let them know that this is important to you and that you would like to gain clarity about whatever is circling through your mind.

If your thoughts are related to money or work, again write them out and then examine them as if they were the thoughts of a close friend or family member. Write down how you would advise this person to deal with these thoughts. Are there people at your job or in your business to whom you could direct these ideas or questions? If so, make arrangements to speak with these individuals as soon as possible.

The trick here is that you are externalizing what was previously only in your own mind. Quite often this process alleviates the tension and stress you are experiencing. Once you have released the thoughts externally, many people experience a sense of relief and the thoughts will quite likely cease to circle around in your mind.

When a person is in action, it is impossible to worry or think about negativity. Action is a positive state that creates positive ions to circuit through the brain and body.

If you are feeling too agitated to do the relaxation exercise as it is described above, go for a strenuous walk, bike ride or other form of physical exercise that you enjoy and then return to doing the exercise.

Quite often people's experience is that their thoughts turn to matters they feel they have no control of. When this occurs think about your reaction and how you would behave should any of these specific matters come into reality. Also consider what part of the situation you do have control over, such as your thoughts and reactions to it, and take ownership of those. Put yourself in the driver's seat and assume control over what you can do something about. Think about what would occur if you could somehow magically be in charge of all aspects of the situation. What is the ideal outcome that you would like to see? The clarity gained in this kind of thinking quite often sends out the vibrations universally, so that situations can unfold much more in alignment with your ideal.

When I come from an ownership position of stating that "I attract that which occurs", I see my responsibility as being "I get to respond to this situation in a way that I choose". Being an emotional, passionate person, I am beginning to notice more and more when I react to other people's words and actions emotionally. When this occurs I tell myself to speak as little as possible and to keep my voice quiet and neutral. Usually I tell the people around me that I will take some time to think things over. I then remove myself quietly and gracefully from the environment to a place where it is safe for me to have whatever reactions are coming up for me.

Once I feel the emotions have been expressed, I then begin to use my mind to reason through what has occurred. This is the time when I most often want to move into a victim position and blame others for how I am feeling and what I am thinking. The truth is that everyone lives inside their own world. What they say, think and feel has nothing to do with me and everything to do with them. This type of reasoning goes far in neutralizing my emotions and assisting me to think more clearly. I recognize what is my responsibility and I get to choose what I want to say and do next.

This level of self-awareness expands as I practice it more and more and it will definitely do the same for you. As your own self-awareness grows, you will notice how your awareness of others increases as well.

Whenever you find yourself slipping into automatic thinking, snap yourself awake by literally snapping your fingers and saying "I am here now and am experiencing only this present moment".

Another technique that greatly assists in improving awareness is to talk less and listen more. When you are tempted to speak, ask yourself if what you want to share is vital to whatever is occurring or do you

86

merely want to have your ego acknowledged. Quite often, my ego wants recognition for its existence. I hear myself say to myself more and more, "Thanks for sharing, but I don't need to say that out loud right now."

Depending on the situation, I decide when and what I am going to say. Taking a breath and rehearsing what I want to say assists me in greater clarity and ease in communication.

## Chapter 9    *CONTRIBUTION*

### *What is It?*

Just looking at this word - "contribution", I began to think about tithing as it is most commonly understood within different religions and church organizations. While this is one form of contribution, there are others. I will write about each one separately and then you will have a writing exercise at the end.

Financial Tithing – what is it and how does it work? Generally, tithing is about taking 10% of your financial income and giving it away. Many people choose to give more or less than 10%, depending upon their own circumstances and wishes. It can be given to a church, charity, family or anything at all. It is completely up to the individual.

Time Tithing - this is an opportunity to give of your time instead of money. Time has become a very important resource to me. As I look at my days and weeks, I am constantly amazed at how quickly time passes. While I know that my spirit is infinite, I also believe that my time in this body is finite. I love the experience of being on this planet, and all the wondrous experiences I have. While I am feeling very blessed, I also understand that giving back to the world through my time and/or money is essential in the circle of life.

I have described two forms of contribution and see that I am now launching into the description or theory of contribution, so will change direction from the examples and flesh out the theory more.

If you take the perspective that the world is an abundant place and that there is always going to be more than enough available to you, this thought opens up a whole realm of possibilities. It is a principle that I am currently working on. As I write the first draft of this chapter, I am attracting an annual income of approximately $60,000 per year. I don't own my own home. My husband works sporadically, on contract, so his income does not contribute greatly to the family household, although he contributes in many other ways to the well-being of our family. I have a 15 year-old son. I have one full-time job, have started my own business with an international e-commerce organization and those are my two sources of income right now. (At the time of editing this book, three years later, my annual income is almost $100,000.00)

I expect miracles and I trust that my income level will continue to grow. Contribution for me is about giving back to the universe and the people in this universe. I feel blessed and wealthy in many respects, not just financially and I want to share that wealth. I also believe the thought that what I put out to the world, I get back. Whatever I invest my time, energy, thoughts and actions into comes back to me. I'm not able to measure this. Some people believe that what we put out comes back tenfold.

No matter where I am on the financial yardstick though, I enjoy giving back. I especially enjoy giving of my time and money in arenas where I see a direct benefit and where my skills and talents are appreciated and valued. Each of us has our own reasons for giving and there is no right or wrong way to give. In fact, what is essential to discover is, why do you want to give and then to decide what it is you want to give, should you choose to take on this principle of contribution.

I am in the process of reevaluating and changing my contribution. Writing this book is a big part of my contribution to the world. In is my hope that this book will become a course or life event that people will attend in person. It is my desire that this information reach as large an audience as possible. Currently, the arena that I am contributing to requires that I sit in an office Monday to Friday from 8 a.m. in the morning to 5 p.m. in the evening. I play an administrative role and it only uses a small part of my skills and abilities. My plan is to shift from contributing in this form to contributing more of my writing, speaking, singing and coaching abilities. (At the time of editing this book I now am a self-employed contractor working as many or as few hours per day as I deem necessary to fulfill my contractual obligations. I also sing at public performances approximately once per month.)

Contribution is not only about tithing, but it is also about how we spend the largest part of our day. So my third example of contribution is our Occupation.

Occupation – how we spend the largest part of the day. Are you a student, mother, father, run a household, principal child-care giver, work outside of the home? Whatever you have chosen to do with the bulk of your day is your contribution. Some people think that their occupation is not worthwhile or that there is too much negativity in their work environment. It is the essence of ourselves that contributes to our environment. Perhaps we are a quiet ray of light working hard to improve a business or service. This is enough. Not everyone contributes in the same way. Some people seek the limelight or leadership roles, others prefer to work quietly in the background and as part of a team. Other people prefer to work in isolation mastering a skill or ability. What is most essential is to accept and honour who you are at your core and that through participation in whatever activity you are engaged in, you are contributing to the world at large.

Every exchange I have with another individual is an opportunity for me to affect that person's world in a positive way. Sometimes it is just through the sound of my voice as I greet someone in a cheerful manner. Other times I may just smile and it is enough.

### Why Do I Want to Do It?

The purpose of this chapter is not to measure yourself against others or to determine the value of your contribution against external values. Rather it is to determine if you, yourself are satisfied with the method or methods you have chosen to contribute to the world.

If you are, and you feel no sense of longing or desire to do more, that is absolutely wonderful and I congratulate you. My sense, however, is that many people are not entirely satisfied and in fact are wondering what this sense of longing and desire is about and what they might do about it. It is also very normal to equate this feeling with a desire for a life partner. I am here to tell you from 26 years of being in one marriage that it is much, much more than that. At least it is for me and all the people I have know who've been in a relationship for at least that long if not longer.

One very insightful Yogi Master once told me that this desire for connection and contribution is about our desire to unite with

Source/God or the Divine. I believe this to be true. What does this have to do with contribution you are probably asking? Well, it's like this. If I take a hard look at how I am contributing on a daily level and feel that some area is lacking, I then need to determine where the lack is. In fact, I am currently experiencing just this. My Monday to Friday vocation is no longer as satisfying or as fulfilling as it used to be. Part of this is that my supervisor and partners in the firm no longer value my contributions in the same way that I value my contributions. My small ego wants to go to battle for what it feels it deserves. The situation also involves another person who was hired seven years after me and whose contribution is now valued more than mine in the arenas that I want to contribute in. It's been stated that my presence is not required. Well, you might imagine how well my small ego took that! Not well at all. I'm trying to decide if the Divine wants me to learn about humility or is saying, "Wake up and Get out of There! Move on and get busy with the work that really means something to you and to which you will really contribute of your talents and abilities.

This is also about moving out of the victim mentality to one of accountability and responsibility. I attract to me that which occurs, so now what? The situation exists, my feelings are valid and I honour them. It doesn't matter to me what others think, or how they think I should be reacting or behaving. The truth is my truth and I get to decide at any given moment how I want to be in that moment.

My highest directive is "To experience, express and embrace life and love and to leave a wake of ease." Will I continue to do that in my current profession? Perhaps, but most likely I will do this more meaningfully through other channels. So, now the action is up to me.

Writing is important to me. I believe that the Divine is speaking through me. I am a receptacle of all my lives' experiences. Learning, loving, being, experiencing, feeling and expressing are some of my greatest passions.

So my contribution is going to shift and change over the next six to twelve months as I move from my current profession to one of being a public speaker, facilitator and personal coach. I love coaching others and have a wealth of experience and connection to the Divine to draw on.

In fact, as I stated earlier it is this longing for the connection to the Divine that most of us experience as a lack in life or a longing or desire that is unrequited. How do we change this? We each have to find our own method. For me, walking in nature or sitting in my back yard is an instant connection to The Divine. Petting and caressing my cat, spending time with my son and small children is an instant connection. Making love to my husband and loving him exactly the way he is in this moment is a connection. Prayer, mediation, and honourable communication with loved ones are all avenues that spiritual Masters and Avatars have chosen over the ages.

Millions of people attend churches, mosques and temples in their longing to connect with the Divine. If you don't know what your method is, experiment with as many as possible until you feel that deep inner sense of peace and rightness with the world. When you definitively know that everything is unfolding as it should, then you know you are connected.

### *What's In It For Me?*

Connecting to the Divine is also about feeling connected to everyone around you. There are still moments when I feel extremely disconnected from others. When the situation of my co-worker being sent to high-level meetings occurred that I felt I should have been attending, I felt disconnected. When I have an argument or disagreement with my husband I feel disconnected. It occurs in life. My choice is to either stay in that disconnection, and try to be right about whatever the issue is, or to breathe, take time to reflect, pray and meditate and yes, reconnect to Source and the Divine. I then come back and decide how I want to be, which includes my words and actions.

When I conclude at the end of my reflections that change may be necessary, I do get afraid. I find myself in my comfort zone and am often reluctant to come out. I have just recently learned that human beings have a bio-chemical addiction to their comfort zones. We are addicted to what we know and what is familiar to us. While my higher self may be coaxing me to embrace what I'm truly here to do, I know that the change may be a little uncomfortable at first. I even become

92

afraid that my financial stability and security may feel threatened. What I need to come back to is my underlying faith that everything unfolds as it should. No one really threatens my well-being.

All of us have an intelligence that protects us from harm. Our job is to be willing to trust. This is a huge wound for me and it comes up time and time and time again. I learned through an early childhood experience that giving my trust to another human being is a very tenuous experience. That person is a mere human being, just as I am. And as prone as I am to err and be less than perfect, so is that other person.

What is much more important is to trust God, the Divine, the Great Spirit or the Source. We are all Divine Sparks of this Source. We came from Source and we return to Source at the end of our physical lives. While we are here on the planet we get to choose to feel a sense of connection to the Divine through our contribution and connection with others. I have experienced no greater sense of moving through pain towards self-healing and peace than through this connection to others, which is being connected to the Divine.

### *How Do I Do It?*

While I'm here I get to choose how I want to contribute to the world. I get to choose in what arena to contribute, how much of my time and money I want to contribute, and even more importantly I get to decide about the value of my contribution. What are my skills, talents and strong desires and needs? What areas of myself do I want to give?

If I am not feeling valued in my current contributions, then I decide to stay in my comfort zone or move out of it a little bit at a time until I am at the place that I say I want to be in.

In closing, please do the following:

1. Write down your main contribution, meaning what do you spend the greatest part of your day doing?

2. On a scale of 1 to 10, 10 being the most satisfied, rate how satisfied you are with your main contribution.

3. Write out any other ways you contribute to the world, whether it is financial or with your time. Rate those contributions on a scale of 1 to 10, 10 being the most satisfying. Should it be financial, list the organizations that you contribute to and state why those are important to you. If it is your time that you contribute through volunteering. List those areas and state why they are important to you.

Now that you have completed this writing exercise, go through and assess how satisfied you are in general with all the areas that you contribute in. Take your time to really look hard at any items you scored less than 7. If there are any areas you feel less than 100% satisfied with (less than a 10), take time to deliberate how this could change.

Do not judge yourself for how long these deliberations could take. For some people, it may take a few moments, for others days or weeks and for others years.

If you determine that you are not contributing in time, money or energy in a satisfying way, explore and research activities that people you admire and respect participate in. Find out what they do, attend events with them to see if this is something you wish to pursue.

### *When Will I Fit Contribution Into My Life?*

For those of you who are new to the contributing game, you may wonder how to fit more activity into your life. Again, look to your mentors and ask them how they do it? Perhaps your place of employment already has a charity of choice or may be willing to be flexible with your work time if they know you want to spend a certain amount of time each week volunteering. For most people, the evenings and weekends are open.

It is not about the amount of time you are contributing, it is about what you have chosen to participate in. Do you feel you are involved in an activity that allows you to showcase your talents, skills and abilities? Do you feel valued? Do you value yourself when you are involved in this activity?

When something is important enough to do, we always find the time and energy to do it. Keeping an electronic or manual daytimer greatly assists us in scheduling many events into our daily lives. By using the tools that are available to us, we experience a much more heightened sense of accomplishment, joy, passion and peace.

While you are making your decisions about the activities you contribute to or research what you want to contribute to, stay in action. For those of you with current activities, continue to contribute and do it with 100% enthusiasm. It is essential not to allow the thoughts and judgments of other people to deter you from what you know be essentially wonderful and true about you. For those of you researching activities, stay focused and committed to uncovering what activities will be of the greatest value.

Contribution is our gift to the Universe. As Divine Sparks each of us contributes to the world at large in our own unique and special way. No one human being is more important or valuable than another. Some of us live quietly, making less grandiose contributions, but the ripples of those less grandiose or outwardly visible contributions go out for miles and miles, affecting people and situations in ways that we could never dream possible. Some people come here for a very short period of time, make a grand splash and are then gone quickly. Many of us come here, live a fairly long life by today's standards and contribute steadily, consistently and with great fortitude. None of these kinds of contributions are more important than another. It is simply our beliefs or judgments that state whether something is important or valuable.

What is essential and key is that you and I are living our lives in a way that makes us happy. If I'm not happy, whose responsibility it is? Yes, it is mine. Who will do anything about it? Yes, I will do something.

*This is the end of this book. Sunday, June 12, 2005 I have completed my first draft. When you are reading this take a look at the first set of pages to see how long it took to get to print and into your hands. This is my contribution and I hope the first of many. Do the same for yourself. Mark down dates of your contributions and celebrate them. Celebrate your life! Celebrate that you are here and alive and living joyously.*

*I wish you all much love, joy, peace and prosperity.*

Lauren Van Kas